KT-166-569

Pen-y-ghent, one of the 'Three Peaks'

Visitor's Guide *The British Isles* **1**

Published by Visitor's Guide Ltd
World Leisure Marketing Ltd
9, Downing Road, West Meadows
Derby DE21 6HA, England
Telephone: 01332 34 33 32 Fax: 01332 34 04 64
E-mail: office@wlmsales.co.uk

ISBN 1 84006 020 4

British Library Cataloguing in Publication Data:
A catalogue record for this book is available from the British Library.

Picture Credits: cover back, Leyburn market and limestone pavement.
Front cover Pen-y-ghent and limestone scenery.
p1, 6, 7(top), 12, 31, 34, 60, 65, 68, 97, 100, 109, 115, 117, 122, 139, 142, 169,
supplied by True North Picture Source; p107, supplied by Richmondshire District Council.
All other remaining illustrations are by the author.

Overall production and design by Isabelle Lewis
Cover design by Isabelle Lewis and Andrew Stevenson
Editorial by Roger Barnard
Proof reading by Kay Coulson

Colour origination by GA Graphics, Stamford, UK
Printed in Spain at Graphycems
by arrangement with Associated Agencies

The contents of this book are believed correct at the time of printing. Nevertheless, the
publishers and the author cannot be held responsible for any errors or omissions or for
changes in the details given in this book or for the consequences of any reliance on the
information provided.

About the author

Brian Spencer admits to having had an affair with the Yorkshire Dales and Northern Pennines
for several decades. Discovering the dales in the early years of their marriage, he and his wife
have spent many happy hours wandering the quiet dales and windswept fells, exploring the
unspoilt villages and meeting the hardy people who live and work in the Yorkshire Dales.

Brian is a freelance travel writer, a member of the Outdoor Writers Guild. As well as this guide
he has also written *Visitor's Guides* to the Lake District, Northumbria, the North York Moors
and is presently working on the *Visitor's Guide to the Peak District*.
He has walked and written *Batholomew's Walking Guides* to the Yorkshire Dales,
the Peak District and the North York Moors.

Yorkshire Dales
& North Pennines

How to use this guide

Over 60 suggested walks, with a
specially detailed selection
starting p. 170, are highlighted
in yellow throughout this guide

The author's special
recommendations are in bold in the
text with extra information in a
green box

*Additional background information
is in pale yellow next to the text*

Maps are located at the beginning of each chapter.
For walking reference refer to:
Ordnance Survey maps, available from all good bookshops
or from Travellers World Bookshop:
Tel: 0800 838080 (quote reference VGYD)

Brian Spencer

Contents 5

The Lune by Kirkby Lonsdale old bridge. p. 40

The valley of High Cup, North Pennines p.65

The cairns of Nine Standards Rigg, Swaledale p.93

Above: Semer Water, Wensleydale p.117

Key to all maps

- river/lake
- motorway
- small roads
- A roads
- railway
- B roads
- peak

700m/2300ft
500m/1640ft
300m/985ft
0m/ft

Dalescape above Airedale p.155

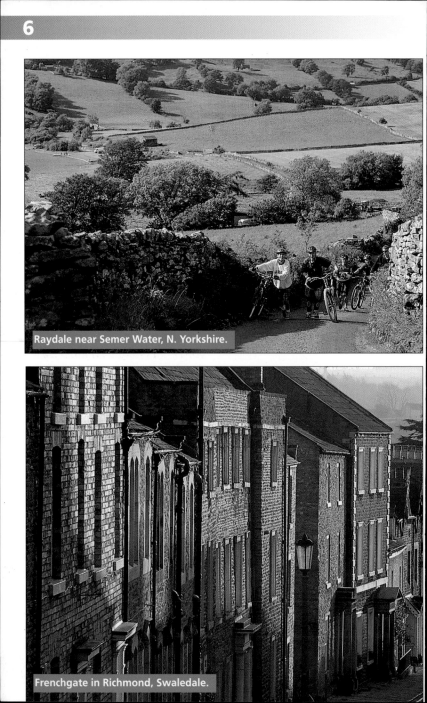

Raydale near Semer Water, N. Yorkshire.

Frenchgate in Richmond, Swaledale.

Introduction

This book is about part of that highland mass which forms the backbone of England known as the Pennines. The range is made up of a loosely linked series of hills reaching to almost true mountain height but keeping mostly to broad rolling moors with an average height well below 2,000ft. Although the Pennines have only a few distinctive summits above this height, it must be clearly stated that their character is closely linked to mountain masses when it comes to weather, especially in winter.

The different character of individual dales and valleys which carve their way into the moors, often separated by high-level roads, is still apparent even with the standardisation of farming methods. This character variation has, to a large extent, withstood the population changes brought about by economic demands or the easier transport of the 20th century.

Top left: Marrick Priory in snow.
Left: Hardraw Force, Wensleydale.

The Pennine Way follows Gaudy Lane down to Hawes.

The word 'Pennine' originated in a forgery produced by Charles Bertram, a professor of English at Copenhagen University. In 1747 he claimed to have discovered a 14th century manuscript De Statu Britannica, a treatise on Roman Britain which said that the country, Britannia Maxima, was divided into two equal parts by the Alps Penina. Until 1822 no one bothered to group the individual heights under a single heading and it was two geologists, Conybeare and Phillips, who decided to use the name when writing about the rocks of northern England and, ever since, the word Pennine has been used to describe the backbone of England.

The Pennine Dales are often thought of as being solely within the confines of the Yorkshire Dales National Park boundary, but their character extends much further north and south of what are mostly limestone dales within the Park. The Pennines can be regarded as starting north of Derby, and include the Peak District, whose high gritstone moors continue north of its official boundary into the mass of bleak uplands between the M62 and Calderdale. Beyond Calderdale the character of the countryside changes slightly and soon the industrial valleys give way to broader and more pastoral dales. These in turn narrow and deepen as limestone begins to dominate the Craven district north of Skipton. Limestone, hundreds of feet thick, dominates the landscape northwards to Swaledale where gritstones and coal-bearing shales which have capped the fell-tops further south, take over.

Across Stainmore and beyond the A66, the broad fastness of the Teesdale and South Tyne uplands differs in appearance from their southerly cousins, but still has an essential Pennine character. This is different from, say, the Lake District or the Cheviot and even the Peak District. For these reasons therefore the dales about to be explored are those valleys draining the high ground north of Calderdale and on as far as the South Tyne Valley.

The Dales have long excited the imagination; Delius, Yorkshire's major composer, looked to the high tops for inspiration and literary brilliants such as J.B. Priestley and Cardiff-born Howard Spring used the Dales' background for a number of their novels. Much-travelled Turner captured the ever-changing moods of the Dales in a number of his paintings and Wordsworth, forsaking his beloved Lake District, was a frequent visitor.

*The hills and dales of the Pennines are not the same as they used to be; change, though slow, is the only constant thing about them. The rock layers which formed the Dales have not always been in the same latitude and longitude known today and once enjoyed a tropical climate before earth movements slowly brought them to their present locality. The time-scale over which the Pennines evolved spans 300 million years, but that is nothing compared with the 4,000 million and more years that the earth has taken to develop. When

White Scar Cave near Ingleton.

ancient mountain ranges were being worn down to become the muddy floor of a tropical sea, volcanoes were active to the north. These formed the basis of the Cheviot and other rounded hills of Lowland Scotland and the Borders. Life in the sea was prolific with countless millions of tiny organisms and shell fish living and dying in a warm environment. Gradually their bodies built up layer upon layer into limestone, often to a depth of hundreds of feet, sometimes around coral reefs, but usually on the flat muddy remains of the ancient, or Silurian mountains.

A huge continent far to the north was drained by a mighty river emptying into this shallow sea, and gradually a delta appeared slowly filling the sea with a fine mud which eventually packed down to become shale, covering the limestone remains of the earlier sea creatures. This action was not at a constant rate and allowed mud flats to develop with lagoons in between. More limestone accumulated in these lagoons before it too was covered by more mud and silt. As the delta moved further south, larger particles of sand or grit were left behind by the river and these in their turn compacted to make Millstone Grit. As an indication of the quantities involved, it has been estimated that the Millstone Grit layers of the Pennines once covered an area of more than 25,000 sq miles and are the results of the destruction of a mountain range 6,000 miles long, 20 miles broad at the base and 12 miles high. As the delta developed, swamps appeared which supported tree-like plants, and when they in turn died the remains were compressed in peaty swamps, eventually – through massive pressure – forming coal.

During the time that these rocks were being formed, the earth underwent periods of violent activity. From deep down mineral solutions were forced upwards through weak points in the rock structure and on nearing the surface began to cool, creating veins of lead ore, fluorspar and other minerals including silver and gold. In addition, a huge sheet of molten rock thrust its way between the surface shales and over a large area of limestone in the northern Pennines. This intrusion, now known as the Great Whin Sill, extends westwards from Cross Fell to the Farne Islands and is responsible for the dramatic crags on which Hadrian built the Roman Wall from Tyne to Solway Firth. In the Pennines it appears at such important places as the waterfalls of High Force and Cauldron Snout, and also in the columnar crags around High Cup Nick.

When all this activity was taking place there was no sign of any of the dales as they are known today. In fact the folds and cracks which eventually became the dales are the result of earth movements which also made the Alps and the Himalayas. These movements were active between 70,000 and 1,000,000 years ago. After this uplifting, rivers flowed down the folds and gradually deepened them into valleys. Later the various Ice Ages covered all, except the highest summits of the Pennines, with huge sheets of ice which ground their way in massive glaciers down the valleys, constantly widening and deepening them. As the ice melted with the return of warmer times, vast amounts of water gave further shape to the dales, sometimes held back for centuries by temporary natural dams, or disappeared beneath the softer limestones to form cave systems and potholes. Sometimes glacial action wore away the softer top layers to expose older rocks as is the case at Malham Tarn where a lake nestles incongruously amongst limestone. The rock beneath the tarn is slate and completely impervious to water. Rock and clay debris from retreating glaciers was left behind to further alter the shape of the landscape and is usually seen in the form of elongated low humpy hillocks such as those found below

Dancing Bear, Brimham Rocks.

Gargrave in Craven and in Upper Ribblesdale. Other earth movements resulted in such unique features as can be found in the Malham area where the layers of rock below the Cove actually started life on the same level as the summit of Fountains Fell some 400ft higher. These later movements, or faults, are again a major feature of the modern landscape, such as the Mid-Craven Fault which is responsible for the line of limestone cliffs east of the A65 Skipton to Ingleton road. The local name for these weather-worn outcrops of surface limestone is 'scar', an apt description.

Gordale Scar, Airedale, was once a cave.

After the last major upheaval finally settled, and the glaciers gave their final polish to the contours of the dales, the pattern known today was left behind. This pattern of twisted and bent folds radiates roughly from a line which starts at Cross Fell and continues south-east beyond Great Shunner Fell. Hills make valleys, or as is the case of the Pennines, hill ranges make the dales. The Ribble begins on the north-eastern flanks of Ingleborough, and to the north the Lune drains south from the Howgills. The River Eden's source is within half a mile of that of the Ure but Cross Fell and the Lakeland Fells force it into a northwards course while the Ure flows east, along Wensleydale. The far northern dales of Tees, Wear and South Tyne originate in a geological complex east of Cross Fell known as the Alston Block. Further south another complex, the Askrigg Block, generates the main rivers of the dales, Swale, Ure, Wharfe and their tributaries.

A winding track serves these Swaledale barns.

The Ribble and Eden drain almost unpolluted into the Irish Sea and are excellent sporting rivers for the angler who can often find salmon as well as trout. In the north the valleys of Teesdale, the Allendales, Weardale and the Derwent Valley have beautiful rivers for most of their length but are unfortunately disfigured by industry along their lower reaches. The main rivers of Yorkshire's dales, the Swale, Ure, Wharfe, Nidd and Aire, all drain into the Ouse, then into the Humber. With the exception of the Aire they have relatively clean waters all the way to the sea.

When a warmer climate returned after the last Ice Age, mosses gradually colonised the bare rocks, in turn creating soil for small sub-alpine plants which later gave way in the valley bottoms to a forest which once covered the whole of the non-limestone part of the Pennines. Trees of the higher regions were dwarf birch and mountain ash, while pines lower down gave way to oak and beech woods, with the limestone region supporting grasses and

Long Meg and her Daughters, ancient stone circle.

(1).The Pennine's greatest mineral asset, lead ore, was exploited by early man and later the Romans. It continued to be mined in medieval days, but the main expansion of lead mining occurred during the 18th and 19th centuries when improved water supply and roofing for the burgeoning industrial towns and cities created a greater need for this versatile material.

alpine flowers. An interesting link with the vegetation of pre-Ice Age times can be found in the shaded fissures of limestone pavements such as that above Malham Cove. In these recesses plants normally found in dense woodland, survivors of those obliterated by the scouring ice which killed off the ancient forests and removed sustaining soil, can still find the ability to live. Here you can find woodland plants like dog's mercury and hart's tongue fern surviving happily way beyond their normal environment.

Man came late on the scene and, some would say, with disastrous results. The first men were purely nomadic hunters able to exploit the prolific game abounding on the Pennines. Their first permanent homes were in caves such as Victoria Cave above Settle where the remains of reindeer and grizzly bear have been found. An abundance of these animals, normally now found in sub-arctic tundra regions, suggests that the weather was not unlike that of today. When later man became more sophisticated he built settlements and grew crops. With this came the need for a calendar to regulate the year, and ensure that crop planting coincided with the correct season. This problem seems to have been overcome by the erection of stones aligned with sun or star rise at specific times of the year. Later refinements led to complex stone circles and possibly the enigmatic stone carvings on Ilkley Moor.

About this time man settled the sparsely wooded and limestone area, and with the pressures of a growing population the initial forest clearances took place, a development which continued well into monastic times and which has only been reversed recently through reforestation. As time progressed, a primitive consumer society grew, first with trade in simple artefacts, then with more complex metals, furs and pottery. Trade was particularly strong between Ireland and Europe and the natural easy route through the Pennines, known as the Aire Gap, between the Ribble and Airedale – a link from the Irish Sea to the North Sea – was on the direct way between the two areas of population. Craven and the area around Skipton became a busy centre very early on in this island's history. A natural progression from what was essentially a semi-nomadic event led to a calendar of fairs throughout the region. Originally for major bulk buying, especially wool in medieval centuries, and hiring labour, fairs have in comparatively recent times become an excuse for fun and games. Only the annual Horse Fair at Appleby retains its original purpose.*(1)

The Romans left many relics in the remote dales, and in fact they would appear to have lived in fear of the wild Brigantean tribes who inhabited the area at that time. They built a fort in Wharfedale on the site of modern Ilkley and quite probably the southern part of the Dales was settled by peaceful tribes. Further north things were much different and their east-west road across Stainmore (a route which is still followed by the modern A66) was heavily defended. *(2)

With the withdrawal of the Roman legions, the Dales, as with the rest of Britain, entered a period known as the Dark Ages. At Mallerstang in the Upper Eden Valley, Pendragon Castle has links with the Arthurian legend. It was during this time that Celtic missionaries from Ireland began to spread Christianity through the Dales. Their usual method was to link the new beliefs into old pagan ways in the hope of gradually overcoming the old with the new. So strong, however, were some of these old faiths that even though their origins are lost in the mists of time, there are still traces around to this day – customs like the Easter Pace Egg ceremonies at Heptonstall in Calderdale, or the pagan fire festivals of the far northern dales.

From the sixth century onwards successive waves of people came from the European mainland, land-hungry, to northern Britain. Saxons, Vikings and Norsemen all subsequently became settlers, bringing their own farming methods, cultures, and languages.*(3) Two of the most visible links with early times which can still be seen around Dales villages are cultivation terraces known as *lynchets*, and the narrow strip field systems which resulted from the necessity to plough long furrows with heavy cumbersome ox-drawn ploughs. Good examples of these can be seen around Grassington and Burnsall, in Wharfedale or near Aysgarth in Wensleydale, and in Coverdale.

No sooner had Harold, King of England killed his Norse enemy and namesake at Stamford Bridge in 1066, than he too was killed at Hastings. This left the country open to the cruel Norman tyranny under William the Conqueror and forced the unruly people of the North to accept an unpopular regime. The solid castles which guard the Dales and command major

(2) One of the native leaders who did not accept Roman domination was Venutius. He and his followers built a fort on the summit of Ingleborough as their headquarters. Such was the importance of the site that after its capture, the Romans turned it into a signal station; the perimeter wall and foundations of several huts can still be seen. By AD 74 Venutius was defeated and many of his followers ended their days as slave labour traditionally working for Rome in the Greenhow lead mines near Pateley Bridge.

(3) Place names ending in the Saxon 'ley' indicate a forest clearing, example: Otley, Ilkley and Wensley. The Danes' settlements are identified with the ending 'by', following the name of the owner, like Thoralby, Melmerby etc. If a church was nearby its name became Kirkby as in Kirkby Lonsdale. Norsemen left the names of features, such as 'skeli' or 'scale' for outlying farms like Winterscales and Summerscales, but their major impact on our vocabulary was to leave words of natural features such as fell, gill, beck, mere, moss, heath, ling and foss.

Bolton Abbey in Wharfedale, was painted by J.M. Turner and visited by William Wordsworth, the lakeland poet.

As the size of the abbeys and cathedrals increased so did the demand for lead for their roofs. Thus monastic orders, who were never slow to realise an asset, developed those lands where lead could be found. This in turn meant more felling of forest to provide fuel for the smelters, and an alternative fuel was sought. Coal found on Fountains Fell and around Tan Hill was mined in shallow bell-shaped pits, but even these could not satisfy later demands and eventually coal had to be carried in along the pack-horse ways which developed around the Dales.

routes throughout the North are Norman relics. Much of the Pennines was preserved as royal hunting forest from this time and terrible punishments were enacted on anyone caught poaching royal game. Many ancient offices were set up to control the forest which, though having no power today, are still remembered and their customs preserved. One of them is the curfew horn which is still blown every winter's night in Bainbridge.

During the Norman influence monastic orders grew in size and importance and the abbeys became some of the major landowners in the Dales. It was during this time that the final clearances took place and forest gave way to hill pasture to feed the growing flocks of sheep. Living standards were improving all the time and monastic fortunes were made on wool. Even the 14th century ravages of the Black Death which wiped out a large part of the population in Europe had only a momentary effect on this trade, and the monasteries continued to prosper.*

In the 16th century Henry VIII broke the power of the monasteries by taking away their lands, treasure, and eventually destroying the magnificent abbeys. The result of this action remains to be seen in the now mellow ruins made tranquil by time and weather.

From about 1300 to 1600 the Dales were vulnerable to marauding bands of Scots who came south, well into Craven, on their cattle raids. These forays were mostly carried out by small bands of men, sneaking into the more remote corers of the Dales, stealing and generally making a nuisance of themselves; the small skirmishes which developed have gone down into folklore as though they were huge battles. A fray in Weardale for instance, honoured by a folk song of thirty-seven verses, was fought between only a few dozen men. The pele tower, a square defensive farmhouse, was developed about this time and allowed both animals and family to share the same roof in safety until danger passed. Nappa Hall, in Wensleydale, and Mortham Tower near Barnard Castle, are two fine examples of pele towers incorporated within a subsequent building.*(1)

During the Civil War the Dales suffered badly in the King's cause. Many of the castles which were still homes of the nobles and lesser gentry were besieged (sometimes for months on end) by troops led by Cromwell in support of parliament. Skipton Castle, which suffered badly, was owned by the Clifford family, and in quieter and more peaceful times after the restoration of the monarchy, Lady Anne Clifford set about rebuilding it and other family properties throughout the north of England. She was an indefatigable traveller who covered hundreds of miles on horse-back at an age when lesser mortals normally put their comfort before any other consideration.*(2)

With the steady growth of industry throughout the north, the move to the towns and cities was never constant, but the effect of the Industrial Revolution was to give it new impetus. The subsequent decline of lead mining caused mass movement away from the Dales. The demand for dairy produce and wool gave stability to Dales' farming, and mechanisation and increased mobility have brought marked changes to life in the Dales. A few villages have declined; some closer to centres of industry have actually grown as commuters make their homes in them. Some provide holiday homes, and most rely to some extent on tourism.

Dales' architecture has been slow to change, and most Dales' buildings date from between the mid-17th to late 19th centuries. Many houses and barns have outside stairs and a few fortified towers are incorporated into later farmhouses. Several dales have a proud castle or a ruined abbey, usually in a riverside setting. Stone continues to be the one constant material used in every type of building, and strict planning control ensures that new domestic buildings are in harmony with the old. Modern farm structures, however, are outside such control and some structures for intensive rearing of livestock are particularly aggressive in the landscape.

*(1) As times became more civilised and the rural population started to move towards towns and cities a more peaceful Scot began to arrive on the scene. Increasing demands for fresh meat by town dwellers made good markets for Scottish beef cattle and gradually a trade developed with animals being brought on the hoof from the Highlands. Many of the old drove roads and pack-horse ways, some of them following Roman roads and monastic ways, are still recognised rights-of-way which can be followed for miles on foot or horse-back across the fells.

*(2) A prominent feature of the Dales' landscape is the vast number of stone walls. Hundreds of miles of them snake up and down fell-sides, pattern valleys and form small fields near old villages. Most are at least a hundred years old, dating from the period of Parliamentary Enclosure Acts between 1700 and 1840, and some – mainly those forming irregular boundaries to tiny crofts behind houses in old villages – are of the 16th century or maybe even earlier.

Countryfolk often travelled miles on foot or horse-back from one dale to another to reach a nearby market. Likewise, the bulk produce of wool, carried on the backs of ponies on its outward journey to the weaver, would meet returning pack trains laden with finished goods for sale, or salt to preserve winter meat. All these ancient methods of transport created their own roads and, where they cross the remoter parts of the Dales or the high moors, can still be easily followed, often for miles, from one linking motor road to another.

Transport has always played a major part in the Dales' scene, from ancient trackways to Roman roads connecting regional headquarters like York and Lancaster. Wealthy monastic orders created routes between their vast sheep walks and granges, linking them with the main priories and abbeys. Later came the cattle drovers whose roads can still be traced, often as walled green lanes.*

The road system began to improve with the Turnpike Acts around the mid-18th century, when good quality roads were built by private enterprise. These roads were a vast improvement on the old trackways and helped speed movement between the centres of population by allowing wheeled vehicles to travel more easily on their superior surfaces. The turnpikes, often built on the route of an ancient trackway, in their turn became the foundations of today's motor road system.

Between 1770 and 1790 the Pennines were crossed by a canal between Leeds and Liverpool, but its effectiveness was soon to be challenged by steam locomotion. In the second half of the last century railways spread to the remoter parts of the Dales. Most of these lines are now abandoned but the most scenic of them all, between Settle and Carlisle, is still open. Despite attempts to close the line, carefully organised counter arguments seem to be winning the battle.

Industry came early to the Pennines with the discovery and exploitation of lead and other metallic ores, and production came to a peak in the late 18th and early 19th centuries. Until then most mining was carried out by small teams of men who would only work proven veins, but gradually the concessions were bought up by various companies, some with strong Quaker foundations. With it the pattern was set for paternalistic employment with good standards of housing, and an education for the miners and their families. In recent times lead mining areas, which declined through competition from cheaper imports, found a new lease of life with the demand for fluorspar used as a flux in steel making. Once a waste product it is now a much sought-after material, particularly in the Weardale area.

The Pennine way enters Hawes through this narrow passage.

Agriculture is the oldest industry, and the beginnings of planned farming came with the growth of the monasteries. The monks developed new and improved strains of sheep yielding more wool of better quality, and specialised breeds appeared in the Dales. Of late, the rearing of sheep as a cash crop has diminished with a reduced demand for home-bred wool and the distinctive local breeds have mingled more with general purpose crossbreeds. Domestic industry such as the manufacture of hand-knitted stockings, once so important, has vanished and likewise few farms now make cheese for sale.

Quarrying stone for building thrived locally at the end of the last century. Today, increased demand for limestone for road-stone and cement has become concentrated in parts of Craven and Weardale. Mountainous regions are providers of water, but only the part not on limestone is suitable for this. The major catchment areas are therefore Bowland, Nidderdale, Baldersdale, the Upper Teesdale and the Derwent Valley, where reservoirs introduce a new element into the Pennine scene. In line with current water authority policies, many reservoirs are stocked with fish or are available to sailing enthusiasts.

A pavement artist finds a new use for old milk churns.

Today's demands on the Dales are more intense than ever before. Easier transport means that more people go into the hills, either as day or holiday visitors, and a significant number commute from those villages within reasonable distance of the major towns. The most attractive areas are unfortunately the most popular and heavily used. Malham, for example, can become very crowded during a holiday period as can Grassington, Ingleton, Settle, Hawes and Aysgarth. On busy weekends these are places avoided by those seeking solitude. The quieter areas are around the Howgills north of Sedbergh, the northern dales, or the lonely little side valleys which no motor road reaches.*

The Yorkshire Dales National Park, in line with other National Park Authorities, is run by a board two-thirds of which is composed of members of the county and district councils covered by the Yorkshire Dales, together with representatives of parish councils within the Dales. The other third are members appointed for their special skills by the Secretary of State for the Environment.

In accordance with the 1949 Act, the Authority is charged with two prime objectives to: 'preserve and enhance the natural beauty of the area' and 'to promote opportunities for (suitable) outdoor recreation'. At the same time, the Authority has a declared policy of carrying out its main responsibilities with the interest of the local population in mind. Obviously, within these guidelines

* With the passing of the National Parks Act of 1949, consideration was given to the setting up of a National Park in the Yorkshire Dales; by 1953 the boundaries had been decided and the area of 680sq miles enclosed by them was designated as a National Park. While the boundary encloses all the major dales, by some strange bureaucratic anomaly, Nidderdale is outside the National Park and the Howgills, a virtually unexplored range of hills between the Lake District and the Dales, are cut in half by the Park's boundary.

* The National Park Authority has responsibility for planning and development control in the Park, but its main contact with visitors is through its 'field services': the warden service responsible for footpath maintenance, patrol and guidance at sites popular with visitors, public and educational liaison and the liaison with local farmers; National Park Information Centres in the Dales, manned by staff capable and ready to answer the tremendous variety of questions which visitors ask; and for guided walks which are organised throughout the summer season.

Wainwright's popular 'Coast to Coast' Walk

It reaches the Dales above Keld in Swaledale which is then followed to Richmond.

For family walking the following Bartholomew guides are highly recommended.

Walk the Dales – 40 walks in the Yorkshire Dales, Brian Spencer.
Best walks in the Dales – 15 scenic walks, Brian Spencer.

Many of the following walks are more comprehensively covered in these guides.

there is often conflict; in such cases decisions are generally weighted in the favour of good conservation practice. The demands of time-share interests, while hovering the wrong side of the horizon, are kept well under control, but the threat is one which the Park Authority must watch carefully if local needs are to come first.

If criticism is to be levelled at the Yorkshire Dales it is the apparent lack of access agreements. Miles of open moors and fell-tops, apart from 'rights-of-way' footpaths, are officially out of bounds to walkers. Several fells have rights-of-way only as far as their upper boundaries where a law abiding walker is left with the tantalising view of the fell before returning by the same path. The fell is in all probability common land, but only commoners with shared grazing rights may use it. It is a great pity that open country in the Dales is not available to all, and it is hoped that the day is not too far away when Access Agreements are negotiated throughout the National Park. A precedent already exists on the Duke of Devonshire's grouse moors around Bolton Abbey. The moors are freely accessible to walkers except during the grouse shooting season, or at times of high fire risk, an arrangement which seems to work well for all interests.*

The walker is well catered for in the Dales. There is a wide variety of accommodation, from campsites to hotels, from Youth Hostels to bunkhouse barns, from caravan sites to warm and friendly village inns. It is calculated that there are about a thousand miles of public footpaths and bridleways in the National Park alone; the Pennine Way traverses the Dales on its route from Edale to Kirk Yetholm, while the Dales Way links Leeds with the Lake District and the Ribble Valley Way traces the river from its source to the sea.

In the following chapters the routes of suggested walks have been carefully selected. None are too difficult for anyone who is reasonably fit. The choice of footwear and clothing will depend on the individual, but novice walkers would do well to read Rugged Country Rules (from National Park Centres). Watch the weather, and leave a note of your route before setting out.

As a guide, this book is not to be used as a constant reference piece, but has been written to encourage both the first time visitor and also those more familiar with the region, to seek out for themselves all that is worthwhile and interesting.

Limestone pavements are widespread in the Dales.

Dales' countryside guidelines

– Enjoy the countryside, but respect its lifestyles, work and customs. Farmers make their living from the land we use for recreation.

– Support local skills, services and produce. Use village stores and post offices to benefit the local economy and help keep them open.

– Consider staying in the Dales overnight rather than making day visits.

This reduces travel and boosts the economy.

– Consider public transport, walking or cycling rather than using the car every time. This is more environmentally friendly and reduces traffic congestion.

– If possible, avoid using your car in the Dales during particularly busy times, for example Bank Holiday weekends and Sundays in the summer.

– Take special care when driving on narrow roads, especially during lambing time in April and May. Park thoughtfully.

– Where available use car parks so local people can still park outside their homes, something we all like to take for granted.

– Wherever you go in the countryside, keep to public routes and access areas.

– To minimise your impact on the environment, select your route according to the season. Try to avoid moorland paths during winter and after prolonged wet weather.

– Follow seasonal alternative routes indicated by National Park signs on the ground. These help to spread the load and reduce path erosion.

– If you are planning to hold a big event using paths in the Dales, for example a large-scale sponsored walk or a fell race, contact the National Park Office for advice on how to make it as environmentally friendly as possible.

– If you are a mountain biker, horse-rider or using a motorbike or 4x4 vehicle, follow the established codes of conduct for your sport.

– Use gates and stiles to cross dry-stone walls, fences and hedges.

– Leave all gates as you find them, open or closed.

– Avoid trampling meadow grass by staying in single file through meadows in summer. Meadows represent winter food for sheep and cattle.

– Protect wild animals, trees and other plants. In particular, leave wild flowers for others to enjoy, and avoid disturbing birds and other animals. Take particular care during nesting time from March to June.

– Keep your dog under close control, preferably on a lead.

– Guard against risk of fire.

A discarded cigarette or the remains of a barbecue can wipe out the wildlife of a heath or moor.

– Help to keep rivers, streams and lakes clean.

– Leave livestock and farm machinery alone. Be aware of farmyard dangers.

– Take your litter home.

– Show consideration for those who use the countryside in other legitimate ways.

– Respect other people's peace and quiet.

Ribblesdale

Ling Gill bridge above Horton in Ribblesdale.

Although born in Yorkshire the Ribble is, in its maturity, very much a Lancastrian river. It has long been a favourite outdoor recreational area for people from the nearby industrial towns of North Lancashire and, as a result, farmhouse and coaching inns of earlier times have developed a tradition providing food of excellent quality. Their close proximity to each other in the Ribble and Hodder valleys ensures a spirit of competition and consequent high standards.

Lancashire's Ribble is a favourite amongst picnickers, motorists and fishermen. Downstream of Ribchester the river is noted for its sea trout and the occasional salmon are caught on their return journey to spawning grounds upstream. Apart from one or two popular places such as Edisford Bridge near Clitheroe or at Ribchester, nowhere does the river get overcrowded, even on busy Bank Holidays.

The road through Horton crosses the hump-backed bridge.

Ribchester
On the B6245, 4 miles north of Blackburn. Pleasant riverside village with interesting weavers' cottages lining the street leading to the Roman fort of *Bremetennacum*.

As this guide is essentially dealing with dales which are mostly in Yorkshire, it is only logical to move upstream, describing Ribblesdale from the sea to its source at Ribblehead. Here the Ribble is well and truly a Yorkshire river.

Working upriver from Preston, the first place of note is the Roman fort of *Bremetennacum* on the edge of **Ribchester**. Roman galleys sailed up the river as far as this fort and later shallow draughted longboats based on Ireland brought marauding Vikings to Ribblesdale. A grass bank outlines the outer walls of the fort, but only the ruined walls of the granary are left of what would have been an important centre at the crossroads of east-west and north-south routes. The site was well chosen to command a safe river crossing over the Ribble, although now a large part of the southern defences have been washed away by changes in the river's course. The late 13th-century church of St Wilfred occupies most of the site.

Nearby **Longridge Fell** is a favourite haunt of devotees of hang gliding and if you want to watch this graceful sport there is an easy walk following any of the paths across the fell above Hurst Green. These give views of Bowland to the north and the whole length of Ribblesdale to the south and east.

Stonyhurst College above Hurst Green is a Catholic college run by the Jesuits. The oldest part of the college

Ribblesdale

M601

A65 · Kirkby Lonsdale

Whernside 2415ft

Far Gearstones

B6255

Pennine Way

Cam Beck

Ribblehead Viaduct

B6479

Selside · · High Birkwith

A683 · Ingleton

A65

A65

B6255

Tunstall

Ingleborough 2375ft

Pen-y-ghent 2277ft

A687

Burton Lonsdale

B6254

Wennington

Lune

Sulber Nick

Horton-in-Ribblesdale

Fountains Fell 2188ft

Helwith Bridge

Hornby · · Wray

A683

Wenning

B6480 · Clapham

A65

Giggleswick Scar

B6479

Stainforth

Stackhouse · · Langcliffe

Giggleswick

Settle

Kirkby Fell 1814ft

Moor Cock

Ribble

Ribblesdale

Ward's Stone 1841ft

White Hill 1788ft

Stocks Reservoir

Long Preston

Hellifield

A65

Forest

Wigglesworth

B6478

A682

of

Slaidburn

A59

Bowland

Dunsop Bridge · Newton

Bolton-by-Bowland

Gisburn

B6478

Browsholmes Hall

Sawley

A59

Downham

Chipping

Waddington

A682

Clitheroe

Pendle Hill 1828ft · Barrowford

14

Longridge Fell

Hodder

Stonyhurst College

13

COLNE

Longridge

B6243

B6246

12

NELSON

M6

B5269

B6245

Ribchester

Whalley

M65

32

B6243

11

M65

A666

A680

8 9 10 · BURNLEY

Ribble

A59 · Salesbury

7

5 miles

31 · PRESTON

A677

6

BLACKBURN

M6

0   8km

dates from 1337, but there have been additions in every century, especially the 19th, right up to the present day.* Oliver Cromwell stayed here, and slept fully clothed on a table during Civil War fighting in Lancashire. The college is situated at the end of a sweep of a magnificent avenue and is open to the public by arrangement with the assistant bursar, to whom application should be made by letter.

The river which flows round the base of Longridge Fell is the Hodder, sleepy unspoilt villages and prosperous farms are spaced along its length. This was the old boundary between Lancashire and Yorkshire and the villages have that indefinable Yorkshire character; here is another world from the industrial towns not so far away, south of the Ribble. Village industry is essentially rural, linked mainly to farming services, but chair making based on traditional methods is still carried out in **Longridge** and **Chipping**. Witches' spells were once an everyday event in this district and these along with Celtic superstitions still linger in people's minds. A roof-high holly of great age outside Thornley Hall near Chipping will never be cut down in case it brings ill luck.

Almost hidden down a side street of **Whalley** are the ruins of **Whalley Abbey**, now a quiet setting for the Blackburn Diocese Conference Centre and Retreat House. **Dunsop Bridge**, together with its neighbours **Newton** and **Slaidburn**, – although once in Yorkshire – are now part of Lancashire, and have an atmosphere that is almost Feudal. Visit the Hark to Bounty Inn in **Slaidburn** and in an upstairs room you will be shown a courtroom where a primitive justice was handed out until more enlightened times. The inn is named after a famous hound from a local pack which had a distinctive cry. St Andrew's Church down the road is mostly Jacobean and has some interesting family pews. North of the Hodder Valley the **Forest of Bowland**, an upland area where jealously guarded access has only recently been eased, presents a forbidding aspect on a winter's night but in summer, especially when the heather is in full bloom, the picture is one of glorious freedom from the pressures of town life. Only two roads cross the Bowland fells; one is from Slaidburn to Bentham in the Lune Valley and the other climbs from Dunsop Bridge to Lancaster by way of the Trough of Bowland. Harrison Ainsworth's tragic *Witches of Pendle* were taken across this high pass on their way to Lancaster Castle and eventual execution.

Browsholme Hall, standing above an attractive terrace, the 16th-century stone house having replaced an earlier timber and daub structure, looks out over delightful gardens towards Longridge Fell. Added to by subsequent generations, Browsholme has a pleasant homely appeal and is open to the public who can enjoy its collections of furniture, tapestries, china and works of art. From Slaidburn the road goes south across Waddington Fell past the Walloper Well (SD 717483) where you can make a wish, towards Clitheroe. Waddow Hall on the Clitheroe road outside Waddington is owned by the Girl Guides' Association.

A little stream flows by the side of the main street in **Waddington** where the houses, each with its pretty garden, are reached by individual bridges. Members of the Waddington family have left their mark around the world; one became Prime Minister of France and another, who helped pioneer the Canadian Pacific Railway, has the highest mountain in Canada, Mount Waddington, named after him. Waddington Old Hall is 19th-century but stands on ancient foundations; Henry VI was sheltered here after his defeat at the Battle of Hexham. The church's oldest record is from 1438 and although the foundations are even older, the present structure is mainly 19th century.

There is excellent fishing in the Ribble below Waddington and day tickets can be bought from the local angling association, or the Red Pump at Bashall Eaves and the Whitwell Hotel.

The market town of **Clitheroe**, now thankfully bypassed by the A59, manages to retain its agricultural character despite the closeness of nearby limestone quarries.* Clitheroe Castle was built by Roger de Poitou, son of Roger de Montgomery, one of William the Conqueror's commanders at the Battle of Hastings. Most of the castle's layout would still be recognised by the de Lacy's, Clitheroe's major builders. Had it not been for Charles II awarding Clitheroe to General Monk in 1660 for services towards the restoration of the Crown, the castle might still be a royal fortress like Lancaster's.

Christianity came early to Clitheroe when St Paulinus' missionaries baptised the locals in a Calder pool, the same pool used for the ordeal testing of witches by King James I's over-zealous 'witch finders'. Clitheroe Church, though very much 'Victorianised,' is built on Saxon foundations. There is a local legend of a battle when King

Browsholme Hall
A red sandstone Jacobean building, near Bashall Eaves, 6 miles north-west of Clitheroe. Home of the Parker family, keepers of the 'Park' of Bowland since 1507. Fine oak panelling and a collection of armour and relics of the Forest of Bowland.

*Clitheroe Castle has what is reputed to be the smallest keep in the North and a hole in its south wall is supposed to have been made by Cromwell's cannons during the Civil War in 1649.

Clitheroe Castle Museum: displays on the theme of life in the 19th century. Small rose gardens enhance this attractive site with its views of Pendle Hill and the Ribble Valley.

Stephen of England fought the Scots under William Fitz Duncan at Edisford outside the town in 1138.

The whaleback mass of **Pendle Hill** commands the view south-east from Clitheroe. This is witch country where stories abound, some true and others of folk origin, telling of witches' Sabbaths, strange happenings and broomstick rides by Demdikes and Chattoxes on wild moonless nights. The villages of Newchurch and Barley have made the most of the dreadful wrath meted out to the poor unfortunates in less enlightened times and local curio shops specialise in witchlore. Pendle Hill in a storm can readily conjure thoughts of a witches' dance, but on a fine day the steep pull from Barley by way of Ing Ends to the summit is worth the effort. A long walk can be made by returning across Pendle Moor and Spence Moor to Newchurch or alternatively carry on to the Nick of Pendle and back to Barley by way of a series of tracks which contour around the southern flank of Pendle.

**Pendle Hill Walk
9 miles – 5 hours**

Old ponds attached to now ruined mills from a time when cotton was king in the Pendle area are well stocked with fish, mostly coarse but often brown trout have been introduced by local angling clubs. Most of the waters are owned by local clubs and permits to fish must be obtained beforehand. A stranger to this area will soon realise why the inhabitants of the nearby cotton towns take such a proprietorial interest in Pendle. All the little nooks and crannies with their remains of old industry cry out to be explored. A small information centre in the car park at Barley will help a first-time visitor find out more. The high road from Barley round the 'big end' of Pendle leads to Lancashire's prettiest village, **Downham**, and then back to Ribblesdale.

Further up the Ribble, the next stop is **Sawley** with its scanty remains of a larger Cistercian abbey, also known as Salley de Monte. Its last abbot was executed for taking part in the Pilgrimage of Grace and many local houses are built of stones taken from the abbey after the Dissolution.

North-west from Sawley a path follows the west side of the river, then off by Tosside Beck to **Bolton-by-Bowland**. The village is set in rolling park-like country-side between the Ribble and Tosside Beck, a stream which starts life very near to the Ribble above Long Preston. Bolton-by-Bowland Church fills a slight rise above the village centre and close by are the venerable

Cattle graze
contentedly near
Ribblehead.

stocks and even older market cross. Founded in the
12th century, most of the church's fabric comes from
the 15th century; note the heavily studded door and the
uniquely designed font which was vandalised in the
Civil War. Bolton's major family were the Pudsey's, their
chantry with its lepers' squint occupies the north side of
the nave. Sir Ralph Pudsey whose three wives bore him
twenty-five children is buried in an imposing limestone
tomb on the south side of the chancel. Sir Ralph gave
sanctuary to Henry VI after his crushing defeat at
Hexham in Northumbria. Holden Clough alpine nurseries
are to the west across Tosside Beck.

Lush pastures between Clitheroe and Settle produce
some of the region's finest cattle and sheep.* This is the
southern edge of the Craven district of Yorkshire, with
Gisburn, its western gateway, a market village on the
A59. **Gisburn** has always been a favourite stopping
place on the road between Yorkshire and the Lancashire
coast, its restaurants and inns have offered refreshment
to travellers since the first turnpike road was built. An
avenue of beech and lime trees near the village centre
leads to Gisburn Hall where there was once a herd of
wild cattle similar to that roaming Chillingham Park in
Northumberland.

North of Gisburn along the A682 and running parallel
to the Ribble is **Hellifield** which provided homes for railway workers on the lines which had their junction a little
way beyond the village. The famous Settle to Carlisle line,
the most dramatic section of a main railway route from
Yorkshire to Scotland, comes through Hellifield although
not so busy as formerly – but at least trains still run! The
Ribble is to the west of Hellifield where it wanders

*Improvements in stock
breeding brought about
specific breeds of sheep
suited to their environ-
ment. The Swaledale
and its variant the
Dalesbred are
particularly favoured
now. The Swaledale has
a grey nose on a black
face and the Dalesbred
has white patches on its
face. Other breeds are
the Rough Fell and
Wensleydale, but the
Dalesbred is the most
common in this area.*

Museum of Steam
Attached to caraven site,
A682, 2 miles south of
Gisburn. Largest
collection of steam-
driven vehicles in the
north. Traction engines,
showman's engines and
fairground organ, all
frequently steamed
during the summer.
Open at all reasonable
times.

Ye Olde Naked Man
Café in Settle was
once an inn.

through flat meadows and at times floods after heavy storms higher up the valley.

Settle is a popular stopping place on the A65, Leeds to Kendal road, both for people moving into the higher dales or beyond and for those who appreciate Settle for its own worth. There has been a market here every Tuesday since a charter was granted in 1249 and the old town hall denotes its importance as an administrative centre for the area. Every March there is a well supported drama festival in Settle, with guest celebrities taking part in what has become a most ambitious series of events. A group of shops known as the **Shambles** dominates the market square. Prominent on the opposite side is **Ye Olde Naked Man Café** which was once an inn. The name and 17th-century sign are said to have been devised by the innkeeper as a protest against the excessive fashions of his time. Settle is busy and yet at the same time a refreshing town sheltered from the coldest winds by Castlebergh Hill to the east, so that it can be quite the sun trap its gardens proclaim. The town will reward anyone with an observant eye; here is a town of narrow streets and hidden alleys where Georgian and older properties crowd in delightful confusion; carved lintels and old signs are memorials to the people who built these interesting houses. The oldest building is the attractive house known as 'Preston's Folly'. Built in 1675 it was so named, because its first owner is supposed to have run out of money before it was finished. The old Bridge End Shaw Mill at the junction on the A65 and Stainforth roads, now converted into holiday flats, was operated by a 12ft-diameter waterwheel with internal paddles. You can see the now dormant wheel from the road. A little further along the Horton road, Watershed Mill is now a Craft Centre.

Coaching inns dating from the 17th century indicate the early importance of Settle as a link in the chain of communications. It was a handy resting place before the steep climb up Buckhaw Brow on the Keighley to Kendal turnpike road. The railway superseded this more romantic method of travel and the line which goes north from here to Carlisle ranks as one of the most courageous feats of British railway engineering. When it was built in the 1870s the army of navvies who passed across the sleepy acres of Ribblesdale must have appeared to the locals like the hordes of Genghis Khan. Despite attempts to close the line, a recent government statement has reversed this policy and so rewarded the efforts of a long and agonising battle by pressure groups. Not only is the line valuable for its scenic beauty, but it is the sole link with the outside world for many Dales' communities. Settle is a popular starting place for train journeys to Carlisle, many of them scheduled as special steam events.

The small but excellent Museum of North Craven Life in Victoria Street, Settle tells the story of by-gone days in this part of mid-Craven. Archaeological excavations in the area have discovered the remains of many animals, some extinct, but others now found only in Equatorial Africa, an indication that the climate of Britain was once much warmer. These relics, the left overs of the meals of our ancient ancestors, were found in **Victoria Cave** below Attermire Scar. Other exhibits of sophisticated utensils and weapons dating from the Iron Age have led archaeologists to suggest that the cave was used as a refuge when the Romans advanced into Craven in their search for lead.

Victoria Cave
2 miles east of Settle below Attermire Scar.

Langcliffe and Attermire Scars are the visible surface indications of the Mid-Craven Fault, a massive shift in the strata of the earth's crust. This fault is in evidence all the way from Malham to Settle. From Settle north-west to Ingleton it continues as the South Craven Fault and forms the impressive natural boundary of the limestone uplands which is most conspicuous at Giggleswick Scar.

An easy walk from Settle follows a path beneath Langcliffe Scar where there is an opportunity to explore Attermire and Victoria Caves. This walk leaves the town

Settle-Langcliffe Scar
5 miles – 2¹/₂ hours

Stainforth Bridge was once used only by pack-horses.

Giggleswick Scar
4 miles – 2 hours

This walk can be explored from a path which begins opposite the turning off the old A65 towards Giggleswick, and climbs through Lord's Wood to a cairn built by boys from Giggleswick School. The path later contours gently beneath the scar to meet the A65 at the top of Buckhaw Brow.

Ebbing and Flowing Well
Buckhaw Brow, on A65, 1 mile north-west of Settle.

centre by way of Banks Lane (beyond the Shambles and Constitution Hill).

Across the river from Settle, but bypassed by the busy A65, is **Giggleswick**, a village which retains an old and gentle charm. The Norsemen settled here and in the 12th century St Alkelda founded what is now Giggleswick's parish church. Most of the fabric dates from the 15th century and it has fine 17th-century interior woodwork, especially the pulpit, lectern and communion rails. Colour-washed limestone cottages line Giggleswick's streets and Tems Beck which is crossed by a 12ft-slab of local slate. A market cross and a set of stocks complete the timeless atmosphere of this unspoilt village, but it is perhaps Giggleswick's famous public school, founded in 1507 by James Carr, with its green domed chapel, which brings most acclaim to this place.

The South Craven Fault continues as **Giggleswick Scar** and beneath it the old A65 – now B6480 – climbs steeply up Buckhaw Brow. About two-thirds of the way up is the **Ebbing and Flowing Well**. On the rare occasions that the well functions, it rapidly drains, and then after a pause refills itself. This is due to a unique double chambered cave somewhere behind the well which causes a sudden siphoning effect inside the hole and temporarily cuts off the flow of water.

A sign at Langcliffe marks entry into the Yorkshire Dales National Park. Northwards along Ribblesdale the true limestone country where the Settle to Carlisle railway competes with the B6479 for the available space in the valley bottom is entered. The first Ribblesdale village within the park is **Stackhouse**, a farming community between Giggleswick and Little Stainforth. A footpath leads north-west from Stackhouse, through aptly named Happy Valley (a popular picnic spot for the locals) to the enigmatic feature known as the **Celtic Wall**. Beyond this follow the escarpment beyond the wall and turn right on the Feizor to link with the Little Stainforth path and eventually back to Stackhouse.

Stainforth was settled before the Norman Conquest and its prettiest features are **Catrigg Force**, high to the east of the village, and the pack-horse bridge built by the monks of Sawley Abbey above a ford once crossed by the drove road from Lancaster to York. Stainforth means 'Stoney Ford', a reference to the attractive scene topped by the pack-horse bridge. The village makes an ideal base for exploring the southern slopes of the Ribblesdale fells. It has several guest houses, a hospitable pub and a Youth Hostel. A short easy walk starting by the tiny green above the village climbs a walled lane for about a mile to reach Catrigg Force, one of the hidden beauties of the Dales.

Quarrying intrudes upon the scene near **Helwith Bridge**; limestone, the material of our roads, is taken in ever increasing amounts from the fell-sides and, to a lesser extent slate, the bed-rock of the dale is still used for decorative building purposes.

Winskill stones near Settle.

Celtic Wall
This ancient stone wall is almost 70ft (23 m) in length, 5ft (1.6m) high and 5ft (1.6m) at its base. Archaeologists believe that it is over 2,000 years old.

Celtic Wall and Stackhouse Walk
4 miles – 2¹/₂ hours

Catrigg Force Walk
1 mile – ³/₄ hour

Stainforth Bridge and **Force.** Below Stainforth on B6479. Elegant arched pack-horse bridge on the ancient highway between Lancaster and York. Owned by the National Trust. Stainforth Force, rushes over limestone edges into a deep, black pool and can be reached by a footpath from the bridge.

Pen-y-ghent, one of the few real peaks in the Pennines.

At Helwith Bridge, further up the dale beyond Stainforth, there is the first glimpse of Yorkshire's famous mountain trio. To the right is Pen-y-ghent, left is Ingleborough, and beyond but not seen for another few miles is Whernside, Yorkshire's highest point, 2,419ft above sea level. These are the 'Three Peaks', one of the hardest expeditions open to the fell walker and that toughest of all sports – cyclocross. The Three Peaks' Walk is certainly a fine expedition for the really hardy fell walker. To cross the 24 miles of very rough ground and climb a total of 5,000ft within the hours of daylight will certainly create a sense of achievement, but only those who are fit and have a previous knowledge of the terrain should attempt this walk. Limestone country is full of snags, from outcropping scars to sheer-sided potholes, all lying in wait for the unwary walker. In 1887, two school masters from Giggleswick first walked over Ingleborough with the intention of having tea at Chapel-le-Dale. Whernside tempted them on and once there, Pen-y-ghent completed the challenge. The route has been run in around 4 hours or cyclocrossed in less than 3 hours, but usually needs all the hours of summer daylight.

There are few rules controlling the Three Peaks' Walk apart from the really important one about doing it in daylight, and the need to complete the circuit in one go. Most people start at the Three Peaks' Café in Horton-in-Ribblesdale and walk the route anticlockwise. The café proprietor has installed a factory clocking-in machine and participants are expected to sign 'in' and 'out'. The proprietor expects anyone who drops out for any reason to let him know as the fell rescue services are automatically called out at the end of the day against any incomplete cards. This also applies to anyone who completes the walk, but fails to clock out at the end. So if you do the walk, please comply with this very simple but effective scheme. The volunteer rescue service do not take too kindly to being called out on a wild goose chase! The route of the Three Peaks Walk is very well described in Wainwright's *Walks in Limestone Country* and it is fairly

The Three Peaks' Walk 24 miles – 8/10 hours

easy to follow with the aid of the OS map. However the following notes should act as a rough guide.

Starting from **Horton** take the Settle road as far as the bridge beyond the parish church. Turn left over the bridge and past the school to **Brackenbottom Farm**, where a clearly signposted path leads up the hillside to join the Pennine Way path, then steeply through the outcropping crags to the summit of the first peak, **Pen-y-ghent**. Cross the summit to a break in its western cliff. Go downhill for about quarter of a mile and fork right in a north-westerly direction (the main path goes back to Horton via Scar Lane). Walk downhill and aim to the right of the distinct shape of Hull Pot. Note that if you cannot see **Hull Pot** either because it is too dark or misty you should call the whole expedition off and live to try again. Continue along a faint track still north-west through, or better still, around the bog of **Black Dub Moss** and in about a half a mile turn right on to the bridleway from Horton to Langstrothdale. This section again coincides with the Pennine Way, but leaves it at **Old Ing Farm**. Take the farm lane left and about halfway to the neighbouring High Birkwith Farm turn right and follow a drystone wall to **God's Bridge**, a natural bridge of limestone, and **Nether Lodge Farm**. The farm road leads down and across the infant Ribble to the B6479 beyond Ingman Lodge. Turn right along the

Ingleborough, one of Three Peaks, dominates the head of Ribblesdale.

Pen-y-ghent
Dramatic mountain, 2 miles north-east of Horton-in-Ribblesdale.

Ingleborough's summit.

road and aim towards the Ribblehead viaduct where a cart track by the Ribblehead Inn turns right and then under the viaduct to **Gunnerfleet Farm**. Turn right, walk along the Chapel-le-Dale track to **Winterscales Farm** and then left, beyond the farm buildings to climb steeply up the flank of **Whernside**. After a rest near the summit cairn go left from the summit and aim steeply downhill to **Bruntscar Farm** with its road to Chapel-le-Dale and Hill Inn. Unless the Hill Inn is irresistible, walk north-east up the Ingleton-Ribblehead road to a stile on the right and start to climb again towards a broad col between Ingleborough and Simon Fell, turning right for **Ingleborough's** summit. This section of the walk across the north-west slopes of Ingleborough is dotted with caves and potholes and is worthy of the lengthier exploration described in Chapter 2, The Lune Valley.

For the final lap of the Three Peaks' Walk it is necessary to walk back along the track from the top of Ingleborough to the lowest point of the col in the direction of **Simon Fell**. Turn right in a south-easterly direction across marsh ground, past **Sulber Nick** and across three walls to a wall above Beecroft Quarry. Follow the wall to the south and at a shooting butt turn left over a stile and follow a cairned path around the quarry to **Beecroft Hall**, then eventually over the railway and back to Horton remembering to clock out at the café.

After all that strenuous exercise perhaps a short gentle digression is called for, and what better way than to comment on the wildlife and history of the area? The most common sound on the high fells is made by the curlew, its haunting call evocative of the windswept rough grass moors which it finds ideal for its nesting sites. Ravens and crows inhabit the high crags and lower down the fells are the haunt of lapwings whose call gives rise to its other name 'pee-wit'. Pied wagtails live in open country near water, but their large relative, the grey wagtail, will rarely be found away from streams and ponds. Of all the birds of North Ribblesdale the warbling song of the skylark brings home the joy of summer as it climbs higher and higher into the sky.

Plant life abounds. On the high peaty tops can be found bilberry, cloudberry and to a lesser extent heather. Purple saxifrage festoons the limestone crags of Pen-y-ghent, along with mountain pansy and bird's eye primrose with the insectivorous plants sundew and butterwort in boggy places. Ferns such as hart's tongue enjoy the damp recesses of fissures in the limestone pavements. Cotton grass and the purple moor grass together with white mat-grass cover the lower slopes between the acidic high tops and limestone outcrops.

Local schoolchildren at Horton-in-Ribblesdale exploring their church.

For centuries the sweet grass of limestone country has provided grazing for sheep bred mostly for their fleeces. Monastic wealth came from wool and vast areas of the Dales were once owned and farmed by the Cistercians of Fountains and other abbeys. The whole of Upper Ribblesdale was one huge sheepwalk divided amongst the abbeys of Fountains, Furness and Sawley. Ingman Lodge near Ribblehead for example was once a grange for Furness Abbey.

The village of **Horton-in-Ribblesdale** is an ideal centre for exploring the woods and caves of Upper Ribblesdale. Try to ignore the quarries along Moughton fellside to the west. The one above Helwith Bridge quarries Silurian

Horton Scar Lane
Horton-in-Ribblesdale. A typical example of green road and ancient trackway still in regular use by local farmers and walkers. Connects Horton-in-Ribblesdale with Halton Gill in Littondale.

Slate which was once used for paving slabs, the sides of rainwater tanks and even tombstones, but now the stone is only needed for road building and to a lesser extent is still used as a building material. Moughton Whetstone was once used to hone Sheffield razors. Beecroft is a limestone quarry with an attendant smoke plume which regretfully appears necessary with lime and cement production. Despite this nearby industry, Horton is an hospitable place, an obvious stopping place for anyone walking the Pennine Way, exploring the maze of cave formations around the village, or just enjoying the delight of the open spaces around.

St Oswald's Church
Horton
A delightful Dales' church built of locally-quarried slate and limestone. Lead on its roof was probably mined locally.

The parish church of **St Oswald** dates from Norman times and is built of local materials from the slabs of its floor to the lead on its roof. Look at its Norman doorway and stained glass windows, especially the west with the ancient fragment showing the mitred head of Thomas à Becket. Do not worry if you get the feeling that the place is leaning because it really is! All the pillars lean to the south and have done so for generations, so there does not seem much danger of the church falling on your head yet! While a number of east windows in Dales' churches have a definite slant, nowhere does the whole church interior lean like it does at Horton.

**Pen-y-ghent 2,273ft/694m
5 miles – 3 hours**

Pen-y-ghent is the obvious mecca for most walkers starting from Horton. The majority take the way up and down Horton Scar Lane, but a more enjoyable route is the signposted path which follows the Three Peaks' Walk route through Brackenbottom Farm from Horton to Pen-y-ghent. From the summit, the route goes beneath an impressive limestone scar with a detached pinnacle to make its way down to Hull Pot before joining the Horton Scar Lane back to the village.

**Ling Gill
5 miles – 2 hours**

Hidden in tiny ravines amongst this expanse of rolling moorland are the charming survivors of ancient woodlands left over from a time when the climate was much milder than it is today. **Ling Gill** north of Horton, is a National Nature Reserve, easily reached by a short walk from the road end near High Birkwith Farm. Follow the green lane to Old Ing Farm and join the Pennine Way which, in about a mile, passes above Ling Gill ravine. At Ling Gill Bridge, which was built in the 16th century, a tablet refers to its repair in 1765 '*at the charge of the whole of West Riding*'.

A delightful feature of the Dales and something of which walkers can make full use are the 'green roads'. These are ancient trackways, often dating from monastic times, which may be traced for miles across open country. They were used originally to connect outlying sheep walks with the parent monasteries and later were used as drove roads when cattle and sheep were driven from as far away as the Scottish Highlands to the industrial markets of the south. The roads, sometimes unwalled, always follow the easiest gradients and best grazing to feed driven animals, or the pack-horses which carried the commerce of developing industry, before the advent of steam. One such road is the track from Feizor which crosses the Ribble below Stainforth and then climbs out towards Malham before continuing as Mastiles Lane into Wharfedale. Around Horton, Moor Head, Long Lane, Horton Scar Lane, Birkwith Moor Lane and the Sell Gill Lane are all ancient green roads.

Pen-y-ghent from the moorland road to Malham.

From Stainforth to Ribblehead the vast depth of limestone is riddled with water-worn features in the form of potholes and caves. This is the realm of the specialist for whom the excitement and danger of exploring the unknown is ever present. There are no show caves in Upper Ribblesdale, but for those skilled in the arts of cave

* Nowadays access to the larger cave systems is controlled by a central body, so membership of a recognised club is essential, but most welcome beginners to the sport. Even though potholing is a fascinating sport it is dangerous for the uninitiated.

exploration another world opens beneath their feet. Even now there are long distance routes being discovered in linked cave systems which only a few years ago were just theories.* None of the caves and potholes in the area are safe to enter unless you are either proficient or guided by someone suitably qualified, but the following can be admired from the surface: Hull Pot and Hunt Pot on the slopes of Pen-y-ghent above Scar Lane and Sell Gill Holes to the side of the Pennine Way path north of Horton.

Of all the potholes in the area, **Alum Pot** is perhaps the most picturesque. The hole is on the lower slopes of Simon Fell to the west of Selside, sheltered amongst trees with Alum Pot Beck falling with a frightening 200ft-plunge into its depths. Another stream enters beneath the surface from Long Churn to the north-west. Water entering Alum Pot does not drain directly into the Ribble but passes beneath it to feed Turn Dub on its far bank. Turn Dub is the tiny pond between the river and the larger Newhouses Tarn above the word 'River' on the OS map. Alum Pot can be reached by an easy path from Selside and Northcote Farm and this walk can be extended to take in the rest of the cave system connected with Alum Pot. A small charge is made at Northcote Farm for use of the private path.

Alum Pot walk
1 mile – ½ hour

At **Ribblehead** where the magnificent sweep of its railway viaduct spans the dark moorland, an interesting introduction to the different varieties of caves and limestone crags of the area can be made by wandering along the cart track from the Ribblehead Inn. Just before the tracks go under the viaduct, turn right across open moorlands and aim for the limestone pavement above Runscar Scar; here you should pass at least ten assorted caves. There is no right-of-way across the limestone pavement, but it is a well used route.

Caves and crags walk
4½ miles – 2 hours

Thorns Gill to the south-west of Gearstones on the B6255 road is a shallow ravine filled by Gayle Beck, the most northerly feeder for the Ribble where moisture loving semi-alpine plants bloom in profusion. Gearstones was once a drovers' inn and the road, now partly followed by the B6255 and the Dales' Way footpath was originally Roman.

It is not often that man-made objects can improve the face of nature, but one of the few exceptions is surely the graceful span of twenty-four arches which make up the **Ribblehead Viaduct**. Built in five years around 1876 by hundreds of navvies who lived in a primitive camp at Batty Green near the Ribblehead Inn, the viaduct is an important link on the Settle to Carlisle railway. Tales of disease and horrific accidents abound from the making of the viaduct and Blea Moor Tunnel just to its north. The tunnel took four years to complete and the work was done by candlelight (the bill for candles alone was £50 per month). No one knows how many men died in making the line for they mostly lie in unmarked graves at Chapel-le-Dale on the Ingleton road. A plaque in Chapel-le-Dale Church comme-morates these unknown heroes, but their true memorial is in the Settle to Carlisle line which runs through some of Britain's grandest scenery.

Ribblehead Viaduct
6 miles north-east of Ingleton.
Since 1876 it has carried the Settle to Carlisle railway across some of the wildest upland country in England.

Limestone scenery above the remote village of Feizor.

Lune Valley

The Lune by Kirkby Lonsdale old bridge.

Some of the most attractive yet least-known countryside of northern England lies between the Yorkshire Dales and the Lake District. The most popular part of this region is around Ingleton and yet not far away from it is an area of equally rewarding country with quiet villages and secluded side valleys which run through Kirkby Lonsdale and Sedbergh. With the Howgill Fells in the north, this is almost unknown territory.

The Lune Valley separates the Dales from the Lakes, yet its river owes allegiance to neither and has a character of its own. Only around its south-eastern tributaries is limestone found, the result of the North Craven Fault. Northwards, shales and a few gritstones predominate all the way to and including the Howgills. It is these fells which feature strongly in the birth of the Lune.

White Scar Cave, near Ingleton.

The river starts its life as a number of becks flowing northwards from the north-east flanks of the Howgills. The infant Lune then flows west and south to be joined by the Rawthey below Sedbergh. The river bounds three sides of the Howgills before flowing south-west into Morecambe Bay.

To begin to explore this part of the Dales we must return to the Ribblehead Viaduct and look through its arches westwards to the B6255 Hawes-Ingleton road. The view on the left is of Ingleborough and to the right the vast bulk of Whernside rears menacingly above Blea Moor. The high country on either side of the road between Ribblehead as far as Chapel-le-Dale is flat, but suddenly the road begins to switch-back and the most distinctive features in the landscape are the tiered limestone cliffs of Raven Scar on the left beneath Ingleborough and on the right, Twistleton Scars buttressing the south-west slopes of Whernside.

The squat little church with its poignant memorial to the men who died building the Settle to Carlisle railway gives the scattered hamlet of **Chapel-le-Dale** its name, and was once the 'Chapel of Ease' for nearby Ingleton. Tree shrouded Hurtle Pot in the stream above the church, is supposed to be haunted by a boggart; no doubt a story put about by revellers returning from an evening at the Hill Inn on the nearby Ingleton road.

As you travel down the road towards Ingleton look up to the left where bare bones of the mountain known as

Lune Valley

N W E S

to Penrith

38

Tebay

M6

A685

A683

Forest Hall

Simon's Seat ▲

Harter Fell 1713ft ▲

Wild Boar Fell 2323ft ▲

A6

Lowgill

A685

Beck Foot

The Calf 2218ft ▲

Low Haygarth

M6

B6257

Howgills ▲

Cautley

Rawthey

37

KENDAL

A684

Winder ▲

A683

West Mostard

Knoutberry Haw 2218ft

Clough

Sedbergh

A684

B6254

Dee

Dentdale

Garsdale

A65

A683

Aye Gill Pike 1824ft ▲

A590

B6254

Middleton

Middleton Fell

Gawthrop

Dent

Dent Station

Cowgill

Yorkshire Dales

M6

Calf Top 1998ft ▲

36

Crag Hill 2238ft ▲

Deepdale

Farleton

Lune

Barbon

National Park

Whernside 2415ft ▲

Kearstwick

A65

Casterton

Kirkby Lonsdale

Devil's Bridge

Clawthorpe

Burton-in-Kendal

Leck

A683

A65

Chapel-le-Dale

B6255

Greta

Skirwith

Ingleborough 2375ft ▲

Ingleton

35A

A687

35

to Preston

B6254

Wennington

Burton in Lonsdale

A683

A65

Clapham

Hornby

Low Bentham

High Bentham

Austwick

Wray

A683

0   5 miles

0   8km

**A quiet corner of
Ingleton.**

scars are still exposed almost as they were after the last
Ice Age. Soil build-up on limestone is very slow and the
level strata allows acidic rain water to erode deep
fissures and crevices into the flat limestone pavements.
Due to the slippery surface of the limestone pavements,
especially in wet weather, walking can be a hazardous
undertaking for the unwary.

Beneath Raven Scar and close by the road is **White
Scar Cave** which is open to the public. Good illumina-
tion enhances the beauties of its varied rock formations,
stalactites and stalagmites and spectacular waterfalls.

Ingleton is a busy and popular tourist centre, which
originated as a farming community, but grew into an
industrial village working local limestone, slate and coal
mining. Water from the River Doe powered cotton and
woollen mills. Tourism started in 1849 when the railway
arrived and crossed the deep ravine of the Greta by a
viaduct which still dominates the town. Man has known
Ingleton a long time, the B6255 follows part of the Roman
road linking their fort of Bainbridge in Wensleydale with
the regional headquarters town of Lancaster. The town
has been well favoured with roads since the Keighley-
Kendal turnpike, now followed by the A65, was built in
1753. Today's tourists bring a good income to the town
whether they stay for only a quick cup of tea, or overnight
at one of the many bed and breakfast houses, the Youth

Left: Pecca Falls, Ingleton's waterfalls and glens walk.

Below: Coins are hammered into the tree for good luck along the 'Falls' walk.

Hostel or one of the excellent hotels and pubs. Ingleton has a very good open-air heated swimming pool and fine community centre.

Ingleton's narrow winding streets radiate from an ancient market place. Even though the church is a Victorian addition to the town, it was built on much older foundations if the exquisite Norman font is anything to go by. Winding Bell Horse Gate descends in steep twists to the River Greta where the cottages of textile workers, once employed in mills powered by the river, fit neatly into the scene. In 1884 influential townspeople formed an 'Improvement Association' to develop Ingleton's tourist potential by building connecting footpaths through the narrow glens of the Doe and Twiss. The **'Falls' Walk** as it is generally known, has become one of Ingleton's best known features. There is a refreshment cabin close to **Thornton Force**, about half-way along the walk, but before that look out for the often missed **'Wishing tree'** with hundreds of coins hammered into its trunk as good luck offerings.

Before moving northwards to the source of the Lune first explore its southern tributary, the **Wenning**. The river drains the southern slopes of Ingleborough, and west of the A65 flows through almost unknown countryside. Collecting waters from tributaries running

Falls' Walk
4¹/₂ miles – 3 hours

A delightful walk through wooded glens follows the River Twiss upstream and Doe downstream, passing waterfalls of breathtaking beauty.

The distinctively tiered bulk of Ingleborough gives clues to the eye of the trained geologist to whom each layer indicates a separate feature unique in itself. To the observant walker who relates contours and names on a map, the lines of potholes and disappearing streams on a flat band almost encircling Ingleborough near the 1, 450ft contour indicate porous rocks, while the complex of streams and the 'moss' north of Clapdale Wood speak of impervious rock layers.

Ingleborough
3½ miles east of Ingleton. A straight-forward climb, but only in fine weather. Interesting archaeo-logical remains on the summit. Fine view point.

north from the Bowland Fells, the Wenning follows a gentle course to its confluence with the Lune near Hornby, giving little hint of its potential strength in times of flood. The old A65 road from Ingleton to Clapham more or less follows the line of the North Craven Fault where limestone sits firmly on top of slate. Water sinks through limestone, but not through slate. Travel slowly along this back road and the division between the two types of rock soon becomes clear; to the north of the road what little surface water there is frequently disappears underground, only to reappear on lower slopes to the south of the old road. Farmers benefit from this by grazing cattle on the more fertile lower fields and running sheep on the drier open fells.*

The bones of Ingleborough make themselves evident on the line of ascent from Ingleton. The town stands on slate and immediately above it there is a 600ft layer of limestone which provides the easiest walking of the climb with gentle gradients and soft grass underfoot up to about 1,500ft. Above Quaking Pot a 1,000ft. band of shale and sandstone which have eroded more easily than the harder limestones lower down the mountain show up by the steepening angle of the path. Later, harder and less eroded shales give way to a final escarpment of millstone grit 100ft thick.

The summit of **Ingleborough** is a fascinating place for the archaeologist, but even an untrained eye will notice the regularly shaped piles of stones scattered around the summit plateau. The first pile seen on the left at the top of the last and steepest part of the climb from Ingleton is the remains of a tower built in 1830 by a local mill owner. Only the curved stones of its base remain to indicate its size. Beyond are two modern features: the triangulation point and a shelter seat built to give protection from all wind directions. A viewpoint indicator sited at the crossing of the shelter walls gives the names of all the major landmarks of the superb panorama visible on a clear day.

Towards the eastern edge of the plateau are the remains of at least six prehistoric hut circles. Beyond them is a ruined wall, said to be Roman, but attributed by others to an ancient tribe known as the Venutians who were besieged here by the Romans. Who built the huts and for what purpose on this waterless but easily defended point, is not known for certain. If the wall is

Roman, then quite possibly Ingleborough was used as a signal station, making full use of the fact that it can be seen over a great distance from Cumbria and well down into Lancashire. Beacon fires have blazed on the summit of Ingleborough as warning signals, or in celebration of great occasions in the past.

South from the summit and away down the shales of Little Ingleborough the return to limestone is marked dramatically by the most famous of all potholes – **Gaping Gill**. The true grandeur is all underground, for at ground level there is just a slippery sided crater surrounded by well worn tracks where Fell Beck disappears. Only the clue to the subterranean dangers is given by the flimsy sheep fence around the steepest part of its perimeter.

Gaping Gill
3 miles north of Clapham. 360ft deep pothole with a waterfall dropping into a chamber high enough to contain York Minster. Local caving clubs erect a winch-borne chair on Spring and August Bank Holidays. No charge is usually made for the descent, but the return journey must be paid for!

If contemplating a trip down Gaping Gill pothole, make enquiries beforehand in Clapham and try to learn what is entailed. Safety helmets and lamps might be supplied, but to be on the safe side try to provide these for yourself as well as protective clothing which you will not mind getting muddy – in any case take a change of warm dry clothing. It will be cold and wet underground and no matter what the weather is like on the surface, a warm drink will be welcome on your return to daylight!

Cave explorers, including divers, have attempted to open routes between Gaping Gill and Ingleborough Cave by working in both directions; surveys show that they have reached the line of Trow Gill from both ends, but as yet the few vital yards have eluded all attempts to make the through journey. **Ingleborough Cave** (also known as Clapham Cave) towards the head of Clapdale Wood is open to the public and is one of the oldest show caves in the Pennines, still only reached by footpath from Clapham. It was made accessible when a wall of limestone which had held back an underground lake was demolished by explosives in 1837.

Ingleborough Cave
1¹/₂ miles north of Clapham. Show cave, easily accessible by footpath through Clapdale Wood.

Clapdale Wood
1¹/₂ miles north of Clapham.

Downstream from the cave the path enters an area of peaceful woodland; this is **Clapdale Wood**, part of the Ingleborough Estate. Although privately owned, the public are allowed to walk along its well maintained footpaths, hence the need to pay a small toll at the end. Little of the woodland is natural, having been improved by successive plantings. Bamboo clumps together with Chinese and Himalayan rhododendrons and azaleas flourish in sheltered dells. Every spring daffodils and other early

Clapham Beck flows through the centre of the village.

(1) Reginald Farrer was the father of alpine flower collecting and became a great authority on the subject. He travelled widely in mountainous regions of the Far East in search of flowers and shrubs, some of which can be seen today in Clapdale Wood. the story is told of Farrer returning from expeditions in the Himalayas and refusing to greet his family until he had seen his specimen plants safely potted and tended.

Norber Boulders
1 mile north-east of Clapham.

Norber Boulders Walk
4 miles – 2 hours

plants bloom in profusion in sunny spots, making the woodland walk a delightful experience. The stone grotto and lake are additional man-made features.

Ingleborough Hall and its estate, together with much of the village of Clapham, was owned by the Farrer family of whom Reginald Farrer (1880-1920) was probably the best known.*(1) The **Reginald Farrer Trail** within the woods as far as Trow Gill is named in his memory. A brochure describing the trail is usually available from the National Park Centre in Clapham. Michael Faraday (1791-1867), pioneer of electricity, also had close links with Clapham as his father was the village blacksmith.

Now that the busy A65 by-passes **Clapham**, the village retains a tranquil atmosphere despite its well deserved popularity. The useful National Park Information Centre next to the car park makes an ideal starting point for a day out in the Clapham area. This is the home of the Dalesman magazine, the most widely read regional publication in Britain. St James' Church, set amongst trees above Clapham Beck, is mostly a Victorian rebuilding on a much older foundation.

Two miles east of Clapham, just off the A65, the village of **Austwick** was settled first by the Norsemen who named it their 'eastern settlement'. It had a market once, but lost it to Clapham; only a restored market cross is left from this time. This is a quiet, gentle village with many attractive old houses, the hall belonging once to the Ingilbys, an important local family.

*(2) The **Norber Boulders** above Nappa Scars can be reached by a signposted path starting at a gate close by the crossing of Thwaite Lane and Crummack Lane. The gate is on the Clapham side of the cross roads. This path continues up on to Norber Hill passing the perched boulders on the way. The source of the boulders can be seen on the right, three fields away towards Crummack Farm.

South and west of the A65 marl, a clay made from ground limestone during the Ice Age, makes the excellent pasture on either side of the River Wenning which flows through the small towns of **High** and **Low Bentham** to the Lune (Lonsdale). The twin villages are more-or-less merged into one, a far cry from the days when this 'home on the common' first held a market. Textile mills were developed in the last century but now Angus Fire/Armour Limited provide most of the employment in the area. The church of St John the Baptist at Low Bentham is mentioned in the *Domesday Book*, the only one in the western dales. Built in the Perpendicular style the delicately carved marble and Caen stone reredos is its finest feature. The fells to the south are part of the Forest of Bowland, here crossed by a quiet moorland road which leads to Slaidburn and the Ribble. Several of the short field paths west of Low Bentham on the south side of the river can easily be linked up to make a pleasant summer's afternoon walk down to Wennington and back.

*(3) The village of **Wray** at the junction of the Rivers Hindburn and Roeburn was once a place of thriving industry with basket weaving and clog making. Silk top hats were also made here at one time. On a rise between the Hindburn and the deepening Lune stands **Hornby** and its castle. *(4) For some unknown reason the castle was not destroyed or 'slighted' as was normal in such cases and it remained a home for many years. The present building was erected by Edmund Sharpe who was Mayor of Lancaster in 1848.

Leaving the Wenning to return temporarily to the Greta, **Burton in Lonsdale** on the A687 (Morecambe branch of the A65), sits high above the river. It once held a weekly market, with a charter dating from 1274 and was famous for a special kind of black potware and firebricks, but the last kiln cooled in 1930.

The Craven Faults and surface limestone gradually disappear to the north of Ingleton. **Barbon Fell** is to the east of Casterton where the tell-tale signs on the map still show potholes and caves. This is still the territory of the speleologist or cave explorer, but the walker can enjoy Kingsdale and Leck Dale and the intervening fells. From Thornton in Lonsdale to the north-west of Ingleton a minor road climbs through Kingsdale into Dentdale. Streams flowing into its beck drain the facing slopes of two whaleback mountains; to the east is Whernside, Yorkshire's highest point and a well used feature of the 'Three Peaks' Walk', and across the valley is the strangely named Gragareth with its rugged cairns known as the 'Three Men of Gragareth'.

Wennington Walk
2 to 3 miles, 1¹/₂ hours

(3) In the 19th century, Wray was almost destroyed when a cloudburst high up in Roeburndale caused the river to leave its banks.

(4) Built soon after the Norman Conquest the castle of Hornby was owned by generations of Neville and Stanley families until 1643, when it was captured by Colonel Ralph Assheton, commander of parliamentary troops in North Lancashire.

(2) During the last Ice Age a glacier which filled nearby Crummack Dale above Austwick, deposited a number of large boulders of Silurian rock on the surface limestone. Subsequent weathering of the surrounding softer limestone has left some of these boulders perched on top of small white pedestals. These are the Norber Boulders, or erratics to give them their correct geological term.

On the north-west side of Kingsdale the level moorland above **Keld Heads Scar** offers a whole series of interesting stones, pot-holes and caverns. One, **Yordas Cave**, was once a showplace, now abandoned and hidden from sight inside a small wood (SD705791). If you take a good torch and do not do anything foolhardy, once inside it is possible to explore this cave. The entrance still retains its steps and the best feature of the cave is the **Chapter House**, a circular chamber with an attractive slender waterfall. The cave floods after heavy rain and can be very muddy afterwards. The best way to get to Yordas Cave and all the other limestone features above Keld Heads Scar is either to walk up from Ingleton or leave a car tidily parked on the Dent-Ingleton road somewhere in the vicinity of Twistleton Lane. Look for an old lime kiln and aim for the OS column above Tow Scar. A hundred yards or so to the right is the Cheese Press Stone – an unusually smooth-faced limestone boulder.

Yordas Cave from Ingleton
6 miles – 3 hours

Above Keld Heads Scar which overlooks the Kingsdale road there is a delightful grassy track known as Turbary Road, unfortunately not a right-of-way**.** This track was originally made to ease the way for horse drawn sledges bringing peat down from Turbary Pasture.

The next tributary dale flowing into the River Lune is that of **Leck Beck** which in its upper reaches forms the boundary between Lancashire and Cumbria. Leck Beck drains the great sweep of Barbon Fells from Gragareth through Great Coum to Casterton Fell.

One word of warning Ease Gill disappears beneath the ground through a system of sinks and in a period of heavy rain they cannot take the huge volume of water flooding down from the cirque of fells above. Once the sinks fill they overflow and the normally dry river bed becomes a torrent, often without warning.

The last trace of the limestone, before it finally disappears underground, shows up dramatically in the lower reaches of **Ease Gill**. Its rock formations and sinks can be explored in a short but interesting walk south from Bullpot Farm at the end of a 3-mile tarred road from Casterton. While the fell road from Casterton is a public road, parking is limited, so please take care not to block access to farm property if using a car.*

Ease Gill Walk,
3¹⁄₂ miles – 2 hours

Casterton Fell can be climbed in a short walk from Fell Road, either by the lane which starts at SD641793 on the OS map or more or less directly from the other end of the same lane close by Gale Garth Farm. Neither route actually crosses the summit, but it is reached by a short deviation about the 1,300ft contour line.

Casterton Fell Walk,
2 miles – 1 hour

The village of **Casterton** is an ancient place surrounded by standing stones and circles. Its development as a wool centre in the Middle Ages led to the building of a walk mill where wool cloth was felted, or fulled, by foot in the soft waters of a side stream to the Lune. The Brontë sisters attended a clergy daughters' school here and before that King Henry VIII stayed nearby at Kirfitt Hall when he was courting Catherine Parr of Kendal Castle. The house is supposed to be haunted by the headless Anne Boleyn, ever searching for her fickle husband and king.

Kirkby Lonsdale is on the west bank of the Lune below Casterton. The A65 crosses the river on a modern bridge, but upstream is an earlier structure known as the **Devil's Bridge** – a graceful triple arched span of unknown age, but certainly recorded in 1275 when funds were found for its repair.*

Kirkby Lonsdale is 'Cherkaby Lownesdale' in the Domesday Book (Kirkby means Church Town). Its church is certainly of Norman origin, but is probably built on earlier foundations. A charter granted in 1272 to hold fairs and markets was disputed, but a Thursday market has been held regularly since 1335. During the 1715 rising Jacobite soldiers assembled round the market cross. An afternoon of strolling round Kirkby Lonsdale and the nearby river downstream towards Devil's Bridge can make a rewarding experience for both first-time and regular visitors alike.

Steep sided **Barbondale**, used by a narrow side road to Dentdale, is softened in its lower reaches by woodland which surrounds turreted Barbon Manor. Barbon is an old place and comfortably by-passed by the modern A683 from Sedbergh which here follows more or less the line of a Roman road. At High Beckford, a little over a mile away to the south-west, the neat symmetrical lines of a pack-horse bridge span Barbon Beck. Pleasant waterside paths radiate from Barbon ranging up and down its beck and through surrounding fields, but a greater challenge is the circuit of Middleton Fell, a triangle of rarely visited fells between Barbondale, the Lune Valley and Dentdale. This is also a walk for botanists who will find many rare sub-alpine plants and orchids growing on the open moorland.

Middleton Fell Walk starts from the centre of Barbon village by the bridge and follows Barbon Beck for about a quarter mile upstream then a left turn through Barbon Manor Park makes for Eskholme Farm. Turn right at the

Kirkby Lonsdale
On A65, 14 miles north-east of M6 junction 34. Ancient town with many interesting buildings. Artificial water course along Market Street once powered seven waterwheels. Five medieval bridges nearby.

The story which connects the Kirkby Lonsdale bridge to the Devil is that an old lady wishing to cross the Lune found the ford deep under water. The Devil appeared and offered to build a bridge on condition that the first living creature to cross it would belong to him. She thwarted him by throwing a bun over the bridge and a small dog chased it to become the first across.

Middleton Fell Walk
2¹/₂ miles – 4 hours

Barbon Inn, a friendly wayside pub near Sedbergh.

Sedgwick Memorial in Dent's cobbled main street.

farm and climb steeply up Eskholme Pike, across Thorn Moor to Castle Knott. On to Calf Top (the highest point of the walk at 1,999ft), to Green Maws then swing round across Long Bank where an improving track leads eventually to Fellside Farm and the main road. The Ribble Bus company operates a service along this road and careful planning will help the tired walker to use it for a return to base. Alternatives are to arrange for a co-operative driver to pick you up, or walk back along the field path (5 miles, 2 hours) which visits practically all the farms to the east of the A683. Middleton Fell takes its name from a group of farms rather than any particular village. Middleton Hall was never fortified and as a result suffered severe damage during the Civil War when Cromwell's troops broke through the west wall of the courtyard.

Below Sedbergh two northerly and major side rivers join before being in their turn swallowed by the Lune, which joins the Dee and Rawthey at right angles. The more southerly of these two-sided dales, the Dee, cuts deep into the confines of the National Park. Limestone has now completely disap-peared beneath the overlying shales and gritstones of the fells – outliers of both the Yorkshire Dales and the Lakes. These fells and their dales have a character all of their own.

Norsemen settled in Dentdale and **Dent** township is a quaint spot with narrow winding streets still paved by ancient cobbles, a feature cleverly repeated in the National Park scenic car park and picnic site at the west end of the village. A few years ago an attempt by the highway authority to tar the cobbled streets of Dent was met with strong opposition from the locals. Its famous son Adam Sedgwick (1785-1873), the father of modern geology, is commemorated by a large granite slab in the main street.*(1) A distinctive sign outside the Sun Inn smiles across the cobbled space to Dent's 12th-century St Andrew's Church. Jacobean box-pews and brass memorials to local families including

Dent
5 miles south-east of Sedbergh on Hawes road. Birthplace of Adam Sedgwick, an early geologist.

Sedgwick Geological Trail

St Andrew's Church, Dent.

the Sedgwicks feature inside, but it is the view from the river bridge of the mound-topped church and the huddled stone cottages of Dent which will make the lasting impression.

An ancient track, the **Old Craven Way**, again links Dent with Ingleton. Climbing out of Dent as a hill road to the east of Deepdale, the track continues across the broad back of Whernside as a well-marked path before dropping down to the Settle to Carlisle line above Blea Moor tunnel. From the railway it swings to the south and makes for Chapel-le-Dale where it joins the B6255, once a Roman road, and follows it down to Ingleton.

High up Dentdale, Deeside House Youth Hostel was once a shooting lodge owned by Lord Henry Bentinck. Arten Gill Viaduct above Deeside House has piers which go 50ft into the ground to find solid rock. Black 'Dent Marble' can still be found in this area; once popular in Victorian times, the marble was cut and polished from a dark limestone to show its fossils which stand out clear and white in outline.

Linked to Dentdale by railway and a winding road, **Garsdale** has no village or township, but dotted the length of the dale are farms which originated as Norse settlements, identified in their names; Knudsman Ing, Thursgill, Dandra Garth, Birkrigg and Grisedale are good examples. At the bottom of Garsdale is **Longstone Fell**, an unenclosed area of moorland popular as a picnic spot, which can be reached by a path from Low Branthwaite Farm to the south of the A684. The view of the Howgills opposite is quite superb and worth the effort of the short climb.

(1) During the 17th and 18th centuries hand-knitting became a major industry in Dent and surrounding villages, the special needles and the dagger-like sheaths used by the knitters have since become treasured antiques. Spinning galleries where yarn for the knitters was spun are important features of many of the colour-washed stone cottages. Their prodigious production once earned the villagers the title 'Terrible Knitters of Dent', a cottage industry which survived well into the 19th century.

Longstone Fell Walk
2 miles – 1 hour

Longstone Common, Lower Garsdale. Meeting point for the geological systems of the Lake District and Pennine Dales. Approx 1¹/₂ hours. leaflet available locally.

The tranquil Quaker meeting house at Brigflatts is the oldest in the north of England.

Draining the huge mass of the Howgills to the north, the River Rawthey soon becomes a moderately sized stream as it flows away from the National Park to link with the Lune below Brigflatts. The district surrounding Sedbergh has strong Quaker associations, George Fox, the founder of this gentle faith, preached throughout the Dales. The Society of Friends have their meeting house in the former industrial community of Brigflatts; the tranquil house dating from 1675, still with many of its original furnishings and the oldest meeting house in the north of England, is approached down a signposted side road off the A683 about a mile downstream from Sedbergh.

Sedbergh
4 miles east of M6, junction 37. Mentioned in the *Domesday Book*. Ideal centre for exploring the West Pennine Fells.

Sedbergh School, founded in 1525 by Roger Lupton, was originally a chantry school linked to St John's College, Cambridge. In 1552 it became a free grammar school and gradually over the centuries developed into the nationally renowned public school of today.

Sedbergh was named by the Norsemen as 'Setberg' or 'Flat Topped Hill'. The hill or hills are the Howgills towering as a backcloth to this town of 2,500 inhabitants, the largest within the Yorkshire Dales National Park. The Howgills, green, rounded and smooth sloped, have a unique appeal and reward the traveller who takes the time to explore their quiet solitude. This is an unspoilt area and except in Sedbergh and nearby villages accommodation is hard to find, but when found, the standard is excellent. The Howgills and in particular one special hill, Winder, have been well known to generations of boys of Sedbergh School.*

Sedbergh has been a market town since 1251; nowadays markets are held every Wednesday on the Joss Lane car park and there is also a large weekly livestock market on the Kendal road. Never growing much in size, it was also another centre for hand-knitting, like Dent. Between them the two townships in the heyday of hand-knitting sent over 800 pairs of stockings to market each week. During the 18th century some industrial growth came to Sedbergh, first through wool and then cotton. Behind the main street are houses, some of which have spinning galleries, but all that remains of this industry can be seen in the gallery in Railton's Yard.

Cautley Spout, the Howgills near Sedbergh.

Sedbergh can trace its history to Norman times, but all that is left from their occupation of this part of the Dales are the mounds of a motte and bailey fortification near Castleshaw Farm to the north-east of the town centre and the parish church which dates from this time.

The **Howgills** and Lune Gorge offer the most dramatic scenery anywhere along the M6 with a broad, inverted triangle in plan, and Sedbergh at the southern apex. Streams radiating from the central point of Brant Fell are tributaries of the Lune. Based on Silurian rock which shows itself only at Black Force and Cautley Crag, the hills have few walls and fewer landmarks. In the mist the Howgills can be dangerous as their ridges and high valleys have a nasty habit of merging and turning to mislead the unwary. The hills are the haunt of buzzards and delightful wild ponies. In the deeply cut ravines and secluded valleys many interesting flowers grow in profusion. The Howgills are hills with distant views, to the west is the exciting panorama of the high tops of the Lake District and south-east the rolling moors and hills of the mid-Pennines. Pen-y-ghent, Whernside and Ingleborough can be seen from The Calf, the highest point in the Howgills. Man has had

Howgills

Excellent walking area for lovers of solitude. Easy walks as far as Cautley Spout Waterfall and Winder Hill.

Another view of Cautley Spout.

little effect on these fells, using them as common land shared by farms around their base to graze sheep and ponies. A drove road came from the north through Bowderdale and crossed the high tops to reach the Rawthey Valley, but otherwise the few fell-crossing paths are comparatively recent. Hill walkers who want to explore the Howgills must plan their routes carefully, for distances are long on these hills. A turning down the wrong valley can result in a long road walk back to base. Careful and accurate map reading is an essential skill on these high fells. Most visitors will probably want to stay in or around Sedbergh and certainly the highest summits can be climbed from there. Anyone wishing to explore the remoter parts must arrange transport at the end of the day if doing a long trek across the high tops.

**Howgills Walk
7 miles – 4 hours**

One of the finest expeditions in the Howgills starts at the Cross Keys Hotel on the A683, about 5 miles north-east of Sedbergh. A stream starting its life on The Calf negotiates a band of steep shaley crags in the single leap of **Cautley Spout**. A signposted path climbs Cautley Beck from the hotel to reach the waterfall, beyond it open fells radiate in all directions from the complex of ridges of Brant Fell. The Cross Keys has a quotation by William Blake over its entrance which described the atmosphere of these fells:

'Great things are done when men and mountains meet. These are not done by jostling in the street.'

Moving west from Sedbergh back into the Lune Valley where its narrow gorge is used by the London to Glasgow railway line and also the M6, there are links with travel of much earlier times. Moving back in time, the first item is a dismantled railway which ran from Clapham through the Lune Valley, joining the main line at Lowgill at the southern end of Lune Gorge. Half a mile downstream of this point the Crook of Lune is spanned by a magnificent narrow bridge, once crossed by teams of pack-ponies. North now and further back in time to **Low Borrowbridge** where Romans built a fort to guard the major route north from Ribchester to Penrith. Strategically placed it commanded natural ways south from high country to the north and west.

To complete the examination of the Howgills one must temporarily leave the National Park which for some strange reason cuts the fells in two, preferring to follow the line of the north-south watershed. The only centre of population on the northern corner of the Howgills is **Tebay**. The village, as distinct from Old Tebay closer to the river, developed with the building of the railway line through the Lune Gap and is known locally as 'Railway Town'. The long steep gradient of Shap Fell was once too much for most steam locomotives and 'bank' engines were based at Tebay to assist trains over Shap. The site of **Old Tebay** village was at one time the border between England and Scotland.* At **Castlehow** there is a motte and bailey, originally defended by wooden palisades in the days of border warfare. The armaments seem to have been sling shot, as a number of iron balls have been found nearby. Old Tebay had its witch, Mary Baines, who predicted horseless carriages!

*When the Motorway Works Unit was built to serve the M6 it was necessary to remove a huge boulder from Galloper Field. This was the Brandreth Stone and once marked the boundary of two nations.

**Howgills North Side Walk
11 miles – 6 hours**

The north side of the Howgills is the least known part of the whole range of these little-walked fells. Tributaries of the Lune cut deep into its flanks, inviting country for the fell walker who prefers to walk untrodden ground. A long crossing to Sedbergh can be made if transport can be arranged. This walk starts from Bowderdale Farm (NY678046), gains height on West Fell and follows Bowderdale to Bowderdale Head (marked as Hare Shaw on some OS maps). A right turn across The Calf and the path over Calders and Arant How completes the long route to Sedbergh. Linking the Lune to the Eden Valley, the A685 road from Kendal swings round this northern side of the Howgills, following a low level route as far as possible between Tebay and Kirkby Stephen.

North Pennines

The valley of High Cup.

T his section is devoted to the headwaters of the South Tyne, the Allendales, Derwent, Weardale, Teesdale and the Eden. With the exception of the latter's main valley, all the upper parts of these dales have been designated as the North Pennines Area of Outstanding Natural Beauty. Its boundary stretches south from the Tyne Gap to link with the Yorkshire Dales National Park beyond Stainmore. Roughly an inverted triangle in shape, the almost totally wilderness area, interspersed with ancient mining relics, extends from the foot of the Cross Fell watershed in the west, with heather moors above the Derwent Valley and Weardale as its eastern boundary. This unspoilt, sparsely populated region enjoys many of the protections given to a National Park. The Eden Valley is also included in this section of the guide as a logical progression between the Yorkshire Dales and those of the North Pennines.

The steep slopes of Wild Boar Fell.

THE UPPER EDEN VALLEY

The group of wild fells east of the Settle to Carlisle railway line, shared jointly between Yorkshire and Cumbria, are the birthplace of three deep and important dales. One is Garsdale and has already been mentioned; another is Wensleydale, yet to be described. The third dale dealt with by this chapter forges its way due north officially beyond the Yorkshire Dales but linked to them geographically.

The River Eden rises on the high fells of **Mallerstang Common** and its upper valley has long been a natural way north and south. Old drove and pack-horse routes cross the gap beyond the Moorcock Inn at the junction of the A684 and B6259. Norsemen came this way southwards in their search for land, no doubt following a route used since early man first began to travel through the Dales. Trains from Settle climbing over Ribblehead and across the top of Garsdale swoop past Aisgill summit, roar down the steep sides of the Upper Eden before entering the valley's wider, easier contours as far as Carlisle.

The oldest way into the Eden is by a bridleway known as **The Highway**. This track climbs easily with little change in height all the way from Cotter Riggs, in Wensleydale, to enter Westmorland at Hell Gill Bridge, a skilfully contrived arch over a deep limestone ravine. Redoubtable Dales' traveller Lady Anne Clifford came this way to Pendragon on her way to view her Civil War damaged castles at Brough, Appleby and Brougham.

North Pennines

With the exception of The Highway, the only other defined path in the upper reaches of the Eden crosses the broad col between Little Fell and Wild Boar Fell before dropping down towards Ravenstonedale. **Wild Boar Fell**, a steep east-facing escarpment is supposed to be where, in the 16th century, the last wild boar was killed in

Brough Castle still dominates the western approaches to Stainmore.

Little Fell to Wild Boar Fell Walk
7 miles – 4 hours

Pendragon Circuit
4¹/₂ miles – 2 hours

England. The only large wild creatures now are the occasional deer and foxes harried by local farmers. A walk for a clear day would be to follow the path up from Hazel Gill Farm to the col between Little Fell and Wild Boar Fell.

Pendragon Castle sits between the road and the river, well sited to command the way through the Upper Eden, but not much can be recognised now of the sturdy late Norman peel tower. It was burnt by raiding Scots in 1541 and rebuilt to its present but now ruined plan by Lady Anne Clifford in 1660.

Starting from Pendragon an easy walking circuit of lanes surround nearby Birkett Common, north-west of the castle. These can be taken in any direction, but for the sake of clarity follow the route clockwise towards the railway then over Wharton Fell. At a junction of tracks turn right to eventually re-cross the railway and then follow a walled lane down to Croop House. Right again along the river and back to the start by the castle.

Kirkby Stephen sits at the foot of Mallerstang fells and beyond it the Eden meanders north-westwards as a wide fertile valley. Here is the market town for this north-west part of the Dales. The church, of almost cathedral-like proportions, has many interesting carvings as well as memorials to the Musgraves and Whartons, owners of Wharton Hall, south of the town. Little remains of the former glories of Wharton, once a fair sized manor house, as most of the original is now in ruins and a farmhouse occupies the site. If you see parrots flying on a summer's day around Kirkby Stephen, do not be surprised – they are the hobby of a local farmer.

The A66 Scotch Corner to Penrith road across wild Stainmore follows, more or less, the route of a major east-west Roman highway. The importance attached to it can be seen from the number of forts and regularly-spaced signal stations which if not always easy to identify on the ground are clearly marked on the OS map. The wild, high moorland on either side of the road must have been a safe haven for the tribesmen of Cumbria and any Picts who managed to get south of Hadrian's Wall. This was difficult country for military rulers to control and the garrisons must have spent many watchful nights and days on the lookout for fires which signalled problems further along the road.

Brough garrisoned the western approaches to Stainmore. The Romans knew it as *Verteræ* and sited their fort to separate the fertile plain of the Eden from the wilderness of the north and east. William Rufus, son of William the Conqueror, built a castle at Brough in 1095 on part of the site of *Verteræ*. It was destroyed by the Scots in 1174 but rebuilt in 1204 and handed to Robert de Vipont, an ancestor of the Cliffords. Eventually their descendant, Lady Anne, came to own it and, along with her other northern castles, set about its restoration after the Civil War. The ruined 12th-century keep and enclosure walls are now maintained by English Heritage.

Brough
16 miles north-east of M6, junction 38, at junction of A685 and A66. A town of military importance from Roman times to the Middle Ages, when it guarded the western end of the Stainmore Gap.

Franks' Bridge, Kirkby Stephen.

Unfortunately the Ministry of Defence has an interest in the fells north of Brough and as a result access there presents some problems! Few, if any, public paths enter **Warcop Fell** and the surrounding moors and any exploring must be carried out with an eye open for Range Boundary Warnings. **A red flag signifies that live firing is taking place – on no account should you go beyond a red flag!** The deep gorge of wooded Swindale Beck which flows through Brough cries out for a path, but regrettably there is no public right-of-way alongside its stream. The nearest which one can get to it legally is along the lane through Hillbeck.

Warcop, skirted by the A66, has many old buildings. The hall is Elizabethan and the church is built on even older foundations although somewhat 'improved' during the Victorian craze for restoration. Garlands hanging in the church are relics of a custom of leaving paper flowers in memory of girls who had died unmarried.

When it was the county town of Westmorland, **Appleby** was the smallest county and assize town in England. In the Middle Ages its population was much greater than today. With the town protected by a loop of the Eden on three sides and the castle at its fourth, Appleby developed around a wide high street which rises steeply from the church to a mound topped by a splendid castle. This castle saw many battles in the Middle Ages – captured by the Saxons in 1388 and later sheltering the locals of Appleby from marauding Scots. As with many of the others of this region, Lady Anne Clifford owned **Appleby Castle** and it was held in the name of King Charles I during the Civil War.

Sleepy for most of the year, Appleby awakens with a jolt in June with gypsies and travelling people from all over the country gathering for the annual Horse Fair, when semi-wild ponies and others are bought and sold by judges of all grades of horse flesh. Paths up and downstream from Appleby can be followed in either direction, but the return journeys must be along the same track for bridges are few and far between. The main purpose of the paths is to provide anglers with access to the Eden, but they still make for easy and pleasant strolling.

From Appleby Castle the view north and east is of the highest fells of the Pennines. North of High Cup the summits are accessible to the fell walker. The army loses interest immediately before the Pennine Way

Appleby
13 miles south-east of Penrith on A66.

Appleby Castle
Rare Breeds Survival Trust Centre since 1977. Domestic farm animals, a large collection of wildfowl, pheasants, owls, some extremely rare. Beautifully laid out gardens. A Norman keep, the centre piece of the castle, has a fine display of Roman armour and furniture from medieval times to the 17th century.

Appleby Walks
2 miles – 1 hour

Appleby's high street and its church.

track from Teesdale to High Cup. North of this point the land east of the high tops forms part of the Moor House Nature Reserve, where free-footed wanderers are not encouraged. Despite all of these annoying restrictions, the huge area of wild fells gives the hardy fell walker many hours of happy wandering.

The Pennine Way comes down to Dufton after crossing some tough country above High Cup Nick and then climbs relentlessly up to its highest point at Cross Fell (2,930ft). Northbound Pennine Wayfarers in Dufton might look despondent, but they can be excused, as they have walked a hard day only to finish south of their starting place of Langdon Beck!

Of all the fell-foot villages nestling beneath the high moors, **Dufton** is by far the prettiest. Its single broad street lined with attractive trees is at its best in late spring when the trees and cottage gardens are fully awake from their winter's sleep. Nearby Kirkby Thore has a Roman camp (*Bravonicum*), but Dufton on a bright spring or autumn morning beats the lot.

Visitors to Dufton can sample one of the best stretches of the Pennine Way by using the signposted track from Billysbeck Bridge beyond Town Head. This follows a walled lane to open country below Peeping Hill where there is an easy path all the way to **High Cup Nick**. The Pennine Way continues across the moor to Maize Beck and eventually the Tees, but do not go beyond High Cup this time. The return journey must be

A Pennine Way Walk
10 miles – 5 hours

High Cup Valley
5 miles north-east of Appleby.
Fine example of a glacial valley. Excellent views west towards Lakeland. Easy walking.

by reversing the upward route. On the way down you will notice a slender pillar slightly detached from the main crags of High Cup. This is Nichol's Last where a Dufton cobbler sat and soled and heeled a pair of shoes for a bet. The 80ft high crags lining the edge of High Cup are made of dolerite, a kind of basalt, part of the intrusive Whin Sill which manifests itself throughout the north, from the Tees to Hadrian's Wall and as far east as the Farne Islands.

On the summit of **Dun Fell**, the southern neighbour of Cross Fell, a number of aerials and radomes intrude on an otherwise unspoilt skyline. These are part of a weather and radar station run by the Ministry of Defence. The service road at 2,780ft is the highest motor road in Britain and can be used by civilian vehicles to a height of 2,480ft, a factor which could encourage the faint-hearted mountaineer actually to climb a hill! **Cross Fell** itself is the home of a rare British mountain plant, the starry saxifrage – *Saxifraga stellaris* – which flourishes in boggy places around Tees Head.*

In earlier times Cross Fell was known as Fiends Fell and was believed to be a place of evil. The name Cross Fell comes from the planting of a cross on the summit by St Augustine to drive away those evil forces.

Just outside **Kirkland**, a tiny village beneath Cross Fell, ridges and terraces in fields near Ranbeck Farm are known as the Hanging Walls of Mark Anthony. They are old cultivation terraces probably dating back to the Iron Age. Scars and other hillside features of much later date are the result of man's exploitation of the fells in the search for lead and other minerals.

Lead has attracted man to the Pennine fells and dales since pre-Roman times, through the monastic period when it was much in demand as a roofing material, and for water and gas pipes well into the 20th century. Its heyday came during the latter part of the last century when the industry became highly organised, especially under the ownership of the London Lead Company, a Quaker organisation which developed a reputation as an understanding employer. Realising that lead mining and smelting were unhealthy occupations, the company encouraged miners to live in smallholdings on the moor edge, with enough land for one or two cattle and a pigsty, as well as grazing rights for a few sheep on the moor. Not only did this part-time open-air activity help keep the miners healthy, but it provided them with additional income. Miners lived in primitive lodgings known as 'shops out on the moors for five days and went home to their smallholdings at the weekend. Thus the five-day working week came far earlier than is realised.

Leaving home on Monday morning, miners would climb miles out on the moors to their place of work, taking with them enough oatmeal and pork to feed themselves all week. Sleeping communally on straw-filled palliasses, a lead-miner's life was a hard one. The company agent for Westmorland lived at Dufton and for a time it became important as the administrative centre for the area.

Prospecting for lead is made by looking at surface deposits, but when these have been worked out it is necessary to go underground. The local method of prospecting was simple but violent. A convenient stream would be dammed above the site under investigation and the water let out in one go. This rush of water would scour away the surface of the fell, giving the miners a better picture of the underlying rocks. The method was known as 'hushing' and bare hillsides around minor streams are usually the denuded remains of a 'hush' which took place probably during the last century. One example can be seen from the Pennine Way track to Knock Fell, where the unnaturally straight Knock Hush stream flows into Swindale Beck. Several major mines were worked well into the present century and the one below Great Dun Fell warranted a 6½ mile aerial ropeway to carry ore down to the valley bottom.

Three ancient routes cross the Pennines north of Cross Fell. The first is the Corpse Road between Garrigill and Kirkland. Next in line is the Roman road of Maiden Way, a side road linking major routes in what was then a military zone. The most modern road follows an old drove way across Hartside between Penrith and Alston. This road, the A686, is often the first road in England to be blocked by winter snows.

Beyond the A686 the Eden, by-passing **Penrith** with its 14th-century castle and prehistoric earthworks, enters its final stage as it flows towards the Solway beyond Carlisle. The final outliers of the Pennine range are rather featureless rolling hills which continue as far as the Newcastle-Carlisle Gap, but the Eden Valley continues to be an interesting place with ancient megaliths, Roman forts and castles to give a spice to the landscape.

The enigmatic stone circle of Long Meg and Her Daughters.

Long Meg and Her Daughters
2 miles north of Langwathby on A686. Stone group with one outlier known as Long Meg, which has mysterious cup-and-ring markings. Visit during daylight hours.

Brougham Castle's impressive remains are at the side of the A66, about 1½ miles south-east of Penrith. Dating from the early 13th century, the castle was one of those restored by Lady Anne Clifford after the Civil War. In 1656 she set up the memorial on the roadside half a mile east of the castle. Known as the Countess Pillar, a bronze inscription and a sundial commemorate the parting with her mother 40 years earlier.

A couple of miles north of the A686 and beyond Langwathby and Little Salkeld is the massive stone circle of **Long Meg and Her Daughters**. This is an oval, 360ft by 60ft, with twenty-seven of a probable sixty stones with an outlier known as 'Long Meg', the tallest stone measuring a height of 10ft. A number of cup-and-ring carvings adorn Meg but the reason for them is unknown, their significance lost in the mists of time. Half a mile away to the north-east is **Little Meg**, a smaller circle of eleven stones, two of which are again carved with cups-and-rings and also a series of enigmatic spirals.

Using the A686 Penrith to Alston road via Hartside as a logical connection between valleys and also resisting the temptation to venture through Carlisle and Hadrian's Wall you can now turn your attention to the valley of the South Tyne.

THE SOUTH TYNE VALLEY

Cross Fell gives birth to two major northern rivers, the Tees and South Tyne. Although the latter officially starts almost in the shadow of the Tees east of the summit, high above Moor House Nature Reserve, it does have an important tributary, Black Burn, which drains the north slope of Cross Fell. The Pennine Way joins the Garrigill to Kirkland Corpse Road a little way north of Cross Fell, just above an interesting ruined mine. This track is followed all the way to Garrigill past the remains of several mines and is a worthwhile expedition from the latter village.

Garrigill, which means 'Gerrard's Valley' is the starting place for a pleasant short stroll along the wooded South Tyne as far as a series of beautiful waterfalls. The walk is easy to follow and starts by the George and Dragon Inn, then follows the Tyne Head road for about half a mile beyond the village.

The infant South Tyne flows gently past Garrigill, which was also once the home village of Cross Fell miners, but now much sleepier and smaller than a century ago. Downstream **Alston** developed as the centre of the North Pennine lead mining areas. Alston holds two records, that of being the highest market town in the country and for being cut off by snow on more days than any other place – not a record to be envied. The market stand is on a sharp corner of the steep main street. Built in the days of more leisurely traffic, this interesting building is rather vulnerable and occasionally gets in the way of heavy lorries. Lead is the reason for Alston's development. The market was created in 1154 for the benefit of the 'king's' miners who had royal protection, but it would also have served the people who lived conveniently in and around the town. Farmers living in the scattered outlying farms only came to market on special days and relied on pedlars and pack-men for their small-ware needs. During the depression of 1812-31 when lead prices fell, the small-holdings were insufficient to support whole families without their men working in the mines. As a result over 2,000 people moved away from the district in a short space of time. The London Lead Company's philanthropic attitude towards its Alston based workforce is recorded by such items as the Reading Room, built at a time when an artisan's ability to read or write was considered to be rather radical in some quarters. Smeaton's Drainage Level,

Waterfall Walk
2¹/₂ miles – 1 hour

Garrigill
4 miles south of Alston off B6277.
Pleasant riverside and gorge walk.

Alston
On A686, 19 miles north-east of Penrith.
Interesting covered market stand in main street. Excellent base for exploring the North Pennines. Voluntary society runs a narrow gauge railway nearby. Shops and railway information centre.

which drained a complex of mine workings five miles away at Nenthead was navigable by boats, underground as far as Alston!*

The Pennine Way runs more or less parallel to the South Tyne and joins Maiden Way above the extensive ramparts of the Roman fort of **Whitley Castle**. This fort held a garrison on the network of roads inside which Rome tried to contain the subjugated British in the uneasy *Pax Romana*. Maiden Way is clearly defined now by the feet of the Pennine wayfarers and can be followed easily from Slaggyford north to Burnstones Farm.

At **Lambley** the Western Pennines can be said to come to an end. Coal appears at no great depth beside the A689, coal which helped the fortunes of the owners of Featherstone Castle whose grounds are now open to the public.

THE FAR NORTHERN DALES:
Nentdale, West and East Allendales and Derwentdale.

The whole character of the northern dales differs from those only a few miles to the south. South Tyne, Nent, West and East Allendales and the Derwent are Northumbrian geographically and politically. The air is different, certainly the spoken word sounds closer to 'Geordie' than Yorkshire 'Tyke'. In only a mile or two an invisible border is crossed and the visitor has entered the remains of an ancient kingdom, for that is what Northumbria was and the fierce native independence still holds true. Now only a fraction of its original size, the kingdom of Northumbria once stretched from the Firth of Forth to Humberside.

The River Nent is short, flowing only a few miles before joining the South Tyne near Alston. **Nenthead** was built as an industrial village by the London Lead Company, mainly in the 19th century. Traces of former mining dot the hillsides between Nentdale and the West Allen which, with its sister dale East Allendale, is a quiet and secluded area with little traffic to worry about. A network of minor roads and pathways gives unlimited opportunity for exploration. Most of the paths were developed during lead mining times and will lead the amateur industrial archaeologist on a voyage of discovery. Abandoned mine workings and processing plant in Nenthead are slowly coming back to life

Whitley Castle
On B6292, 2 miles north of Alston. Fine example of a well fortified Roman fort. No public access, but footpaths from the B6292 pass either side.

Maiden Way Walk
6 miles – 3 hours

British Rail abandoned Alston, but when the railway still linked with the main line at Haltwhistle two-coach diesel trains, delightfully named as Bobby Shaftoe and Coffee Johnny, plied up and down every hour or so. The line served a valley community and often during winter storms it was the only link with the outside world.

Nenthead Mines and Museum
Nenthead, on B6293 Reconstructed lead mining complex. Trails and interpretive plaques.

Nentsberry Mining and Farming Museum
Narrow gauge railway; play area, picnic site. Pub nearby.

as a visitor centre, with trails and interpretive boards to explain the complex layout of the ore-crushing plant and smelters. About 1¹/₂ miles down the road from Nenthead, a small museum at **Nentsberry** houses a collection of old mining equipment and farming implements, together with a children's play area and a narrow gauge mineral railway.*

Derwentdale, the last of five dales of the far North Pennines, cuts around Consett, now recovering from the decline of Britain's steel industry. The Derwent born in the wild moorland of Redburn Common is not far from the source of the Wear. For most of its infancy the Derwent flows through a rocky tree-lined gorge known as the Sweep, before slowing into the artificial lake of **Derwent Reservoir**. Used as an amenity the reservoir is available for sailing enthusiasts and is well stocked with trout. **Blanchland**, the first village in the upper valley, is a picture-postcard place. Part of the Crewe estate (the village pub is the Lord Crewe Arms), Blanchland was rebuilt in the 18th century to house lead miners on the site of the abbey. Blanchland means 'White Land' after the white Premonstratensian canons who founded the abbey in 1165. After the Dissolution of the Monasteries the monks were driven away but the church was spared and remains as the village church. As with many old churches, Blanchland's was renovated in the 19th century and little remains of its ancient fabric apart from the tower and north transept.

Edmondbyers to the south of the reservoir has an attractive church which dates from Norman times although much of what is seen now is the result of 19th-century restoration. It once had two pubs but only one retains its licence, the other having been converted into a Youth Hostel.

WEARDALE

South now into Weardale and into the County Palatine of Durham, once a kingdom and still a bishopric. The Wear, has created a valley of character but, unlike the wholly Yorkshire rivers, it flows to the sea in its own right.

Killhope Burn, the Wear's first tributary, rises only a mile or so away from Nenthead and in earlier times provided power to drive a massive 40ft-diameter waterwheel at **Killhope**. The wheel and ore-crushing shed of

New Year's Eve is honoured in Allendale Town by a strange custom with 'Guizers', dressed in a mixture of eastern and medieval clothes parading through the village with barrels of blazing tar on their heads. When they reach the market place, they throw the barrels onto a bonfire and after midnight go round local houses 'first footing'. This pagan custom is thought to be linked with a Viking festival brought to the valley by the first settlers.

Derwent Reservoir
B6306, 7 miles north-west of Consett. Fishing, sailing, picnic areas. Pow Hill Country Park and Nature Reserve.

Blanchland
B6306, 4 miles west of Edmondbyers. Site of 12th-century abbey of the White Friars. Now mainly a mid-18th-century estate village.

Killhope Wheel Lead Mining Centre
2¹/₄ miles east of Nenthead on B6293 in Upper Weardale. Well preserved iron 'overshot' waterwheel fed by nearby streams.

1840 still stand in splendid isolation on the moor's edge, testimony to the work involved in producing metal from lead ore. The wheel and its attendant buildings have been refurbished to provide an interpretive centre in what was a highly industrialised area. A miners' 'shop' or bunkhouse shows a little of the spartan life of this not-so-long-dead industry and a Dales' pony demonstrates its usefulness to lead miners.

The 40ft-diameter waterwheel at Killhope.

The stream runs on purposefully through Weardale Forest. Linking with Burnhope Burn below the village of Cowshill, the Wear loses some of its mountain wilderness, and is later fed by three more major side streams before flowing on through an ever widening valley beyond Wolsingham.

The spread of hamlets and smallholdings in Upper Weardale is typical of the way mining communities developed at the height of the lead mining industry. Apart from the refurbished mining complex of Killhope Wheel there is little to indicate the onetime mining activity.

St John's Chapel, in Cowshill (its full title is St John Weardale) has a relaxed atmosphere, far removed from the time when it was necessary to form a vigilante group known as 'The Association for the Prosecution of Felons and other Offenders'. This group still survives but, leaving the law in proper hands, devotes itself to an annual get-together.

Cowshill at the junction of the A689 valley road with the B6295 from Allendale Town is typical of the stone-built villages of Upper Weardale.* The squat church tower looks out over a village green and a diminutive classical town hall formalises this 'capital' of Upper Weardale. Friendly inns serve the needs of farmers attending the frequent cattle and sheep markets. An agricultural show and a music festival are the highlights of a busy calendar. The tiny nearby hamlet of **Daddry Shield** once hosted cockfights but is now a law-abiding group of pretty whitewashed cottages.

Beyond Eastgate the obtrusive dust from a cement works rises from a tall chimney and cement dust covers the surrounding walls and hedges, but fortunately the majestic moors rising steeply on all sides rapidly compensate for this intrusion. **Eastgate** was the gatehouse of the Bishop of Durham's Old Park hunting ground; **Westgate** marks the western boundary. Much earlier the whole area around Weardale was popular sporting ground for the Roman upper classes in northern Britain. Edward III had a confrontation with the Scots on the moors above Eastgate in 1327, but luckily the Scots withdrew before either side drew blood.

Westernhopeburn, on the side road between Eastgate and Westgate, is one of the least altered farmhouses in Weardale. Dated 1601, it is one continuous low stone structure in the medieval style, built to house animals and family under one roof.

A side dale, Rookhope, joins the Wear at Eastgate and the only access is by a narrow road climbing the valley. It is difficult to imagine that **Rookhope** was once an industrial village, the centre of a large lead and ironstone mining area. From the now abandoned lead smelter at Lintzgarth a 2-mile long flue climbed to Redburn Common where poisoned vegetation is still struggling to recover. A railway, now part of the Waskerley Way footpath, climbed high across Stanhope's moors to Consett. Rowley Station near Consett, or Waskerley Station on the moors (NZ052454) are good access points for the Waskerley Way, with plenty of car parking space. Steep gradients were negotiated by inclined planes and hauling cables powered by fixed winding engines.

Rookhope Dale was the scene of a border battle commemorated in a long and not easily followed song of thirty-seven verses.*

In the Middle Ages the discovery of iron ore in Weardale led to the development of small forges, but with the coming of the Industrial Revolution there was an ever increasing demand for good quality iron. Ore which was mined in the higher valley at Cowshill and Ireshopeburn was transported to a blast furnace built in 1845 at Stanhope. Building the furnace there took advantage not only of nearby ironstone, but limestone, a necessary ingredient in the production of iron. The other essential ingredient was brought in on the rapidly developing railway network from the Durham coalfields further east. As demand for iron increased the Weardale Iron Company was formed, which built a further six blast furnaces at Tow Law lower down the Valley. As lead mining declined there was an ever growing concentration

*In the 16th century Moss Troopers of North Tyne and Cheviot ranged far and wide in lawless pursuit of other people's cattle and sheep. Thinking Weardale would give them easy pickings a hundred Moss Troopers came over from Tynedale to drive Weardale cattle and sheep into Rookhope Dale. A small band of locals pursued them and a fierce battle took place on Nookton Edge where the hundred raiders were defeated by forty locals.

on mining ironstone and at one time 1,700 men were employed in the local industry. From those humble beginnings the north-eastern steel industry developed, gradually moving further eastwards and culminating with a massive investment at Consett. Since the drastic reorganisation of the iron and steel industry, Consett's furnaces no longer stain the night sky red and the complex site has been cleared. Stanhope has also lost its ironstone links, but its limestone industry thrives, now producing cement and roadstone.

Stanhope has been called the 'capital of Weardale', a high accolade for a small town, but certainly it marks the transition between encroaching industrial Durham and the wild fells on either side of the upper dale. Prosperity founded on its early lead connections made the ecclesiastical living wealthy and as a result Stanhope has had a long line of eminent rectors, eight of whom became bishops. The church dates from the 12th century and inside it are two Flemish panel paintings and a Roman altar found on **Bollihope Common** in 1747. *

As there are no evident Roman remains on Bollihope it is pure conjecture to try and guess how the altar came to be there in the first place, but a possible clue is shown on the OS map. This is the mention of Bollihope Spa a little to the east of Bollihope Carrs (1,773ft) about 5 miles south-west of Stanhope. One can only surmise that maybe there is a Roman bath somewhere around Bollihope Spa, for they had a knack of being able to find suitable springs and Roman baths have been found in less likely places.

The mock castle at the side of Stanhope's market square is a rather forbidding place, once used as a remand home. Now flats, it was built in 1798 for Cuthbert Rippon, MP for Gateshead. Despite its unattractive appearance from the street, the castle looks much better from the river. The oldest part of the town sits back from the irregular shaped market square and its ancient cross, but far older is the fossilised tree stump built into the church wall.

Two more attractive side dales join the Upper Wear, the first **Bollihope Burn** joins the main river below Frosterley. A special form of limestone speckled by thousands of fossils has been quarried nearby for hundreds of years. Known as Frosterley black marble, and much favoured by Victorians, there is a line of it in Durham Cathedral which marks the point beyond which women were once forbidden to pass. The village gained a mention in the Bolden Beuk, the 1183 equivalent of the Domesday Book.

Tree-lined **Waskerley Beck** flows through **Wolsingham**, a pleasant blend of industry and rural cottages. One or two buildings are of special merit; 18th-century Whitfield House has an almost French provincial air. Next to it and in complete contrast is Whitfield Place, a 17th-century house with mullioned windows. The church tower is 12th-century, but the rest is in mid-Victorian early English style. Wolsingham holds an annual show the first weekend in September, an ambitious event for such a small place. The Wear provides good trout and salmon fishing and Tunstall Reservoir above the town is stocked with both brown and rainbow trout. Rod licences and day permits can be bought locally.

Hamsterley Forest, reached along minor roads south of Wolsingham, has a short but pleasant forest drive (toll road) and several interesting walking trails and picnic sites. Downstream from Wolsingham heavy industry makes itself felt, even in this ancient town, founded in the seventh century during an expansion westwards by Angles under King Edwin of Northumbria (AD616-632). Place names ending in 'ham', such as Wolsingham, indicate a homestead or a small farm which was built in a clearing in what would at that time have been dense forest. Wolsingham marks the end of the narrowest part of the dale for beyond this point the Wear begins to meander south-east, almost to Bishop Auckland, before turning north past the magnificent cathedral city of Durham, then out through the industrial plain towards Sunderland and the North Sea.

North of England Open-Air Museum
Beamish, off A693, Stanley to Chester-le-Street road.
A 200-acre open-air museum of northern life. Includes a 1920s town street with shops, houses, pub, colliery etc. Also a working farm, working replica of early locomotives, tram track, and other exhibits.

Weardale Folk Museum
High House, Ireshopeburn (A689) Farming and geology displays. Interesting chapel associated with John Wesley, next door.

Mallerstang Fells are wild and little visited.

Teesdale

Teesdale is now wholly within County Durham, but it has an ambience which relates it to the Yorkshire Dales. The Tees in its upper reaches is the most boisterous of Pennine rivers, even though man has tried to tame it in its infancy. Cow Green Reservoir was built to serve industry, and in so doing altered the face of one of the wildest areas of northern moorland. From its magnificent beginnings in the hills, the Tees eventually becomes the servant of man on industrial Teesside. Fortunately this guide is only interested in its Pennine life, and here is ample recompense for the industrial horrors further east.

The imposing Bowes Museum, near Barnard Castle.

High Force thunders over the Whin Sill.

*Alpine flowers grow well in Upper Teesdale on a soil based on sugar limestone. This stone was made by the action of heat on hard limestone during the time when molten dolerite was flowing between ancient layers of limestone to form the Whin Sill. Sugar limestone crumbles into an alkaline dust which, when mixed naturally with peaty loam, forms an ideal growing medium for delicate plants usually found in mountainous regions.

From Barnard Castle, which marks the end of the division between fell and plain, a quiet motor road running north-westwards (the B6277) follows the river until they part company above High Force. Beyond this point the road continues to climb to 1,862ft over Harwood Common on its way to Alston and the South Tyne. This road is a delight to motorists in summer when the ever-changing views range from the wooded beauty of the dale above Middleton, to the far-ranging prospect across West Common towards the birthplace of the Tees high on Cross Fell.

Tees Head is in fact a swamp situated at 2,532ft beneath the final 400ft of Cross Fell and is crossed with care by hundreds of walkers who explore the Pennine Way every year. The area of bleak moorland east of Cross Fell through which the infant river threads its course is the National Nature Reserve of Moor House. It is an area of jealously preserved unspoilt moors and contains a unique collection of the sub-arctic flora which can cope with a growing season of only 165 days. These plants range from the starry saxifrage which blossoms in the mossy places around Tees Head to the beautiful spring gentian (*verna*) found lower down the valley. * So special is this flower to Teesdale that a gentian watch is kept over it by volunteers

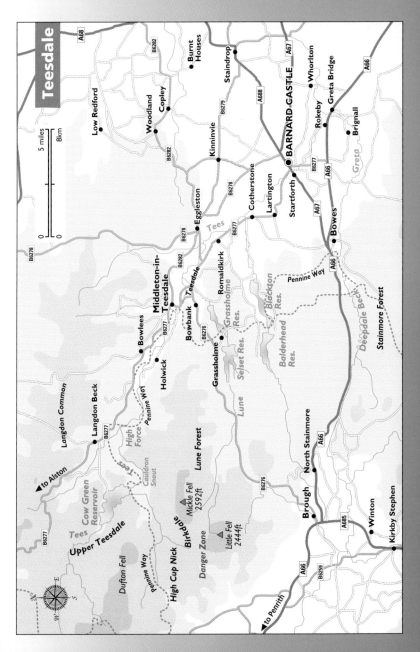

Cauldron Snout Waterfall
Cow Green, access by track from Wheelhead Syke Car Park.

Wheelhead Syke Nature Trail
Cow Green Reservoir, approached from Langdon Beck off B6277. Scenic car park above reservoir. Nature trail leads from car park across moorland. Opportunity to see spring gentians flowering.

during the flowering season. To find this startling blue flower is pure delight. **Moor House**, the home and centre of this reserve, is locked in a bend of the Tees above its junction with Trout Beck; courses are run from here and studies funded by the Nature Conservancy. Moor House is in a lonely and secluded spot at the end of the road which follows the South Tyne through Garrigill to its head waters.

Downstream from Moor House, the Tees is temporarily arrested by **Cow Green Reservoir**. When the proposal was made to dam this section of the valley the industrialists no doubt thought they had an easy task; to them this was just a piece of wilderness which no one wanted. How wrong they were! The battle to save Cow Green was long and acrimonious. In the end the ranks of Mammon won the day, but they were forced to delay the construction of the dam long enough to allow conservationists time to mount a massive campaign to dig up as many of the rare plants as possible, and transplant them in suitable locations away from the reservoir. Despite the heartache when Cow Green was flooded, the lake now makes an attractive foreground to the heights of Dun Fell and Cross Fell, but even so it is man-made and an intruder in this special place.

Immediately below Cow Green dam the dark coloured dolerite crag of Whin Sill resists the river and makes an impressive foundation to **Cauldron Snout**. The construction of the dam means that Cauldron Snout can never again be the angry mass of cream and brown foam after heavy rain. However, Cauldron Snout is now accessible by the road to the dam from Langdon Beck. Cars must be parked at Wheelhead Syke and the road marked by an interesting nature trail follows the side of the reservoir to the dam; a little way beyond it is Cauldron Snout.

Below Cauldron Snout the Tees is joined by Maize Beck and about a mile upstream **Birkdale** is probably the most remote farmstead in England. Winters can be so severe and long that the farmer and his wife once had to buy a snow scooter to keep in contact with civilisation and, more importantly, to check on any sheep trapped under snowdrifts.

The Pennine Way path cuts a corner off Maize Beck on its way over to High Cup Nick and Dufton. Beyond Birkdale and marked on the map is a ruin known as **Moss Shop**, where miners would live for five days each week,

Upper Teesdale.

sleeping on lice-infested straw-filled sacks and living on a diet of oatmeal, pork and potatoes. Similar hovels which dot the North Pennine hillsides speak evocatively of the hard life led by miners a century or so ago.

The **Langdon Beck** district is a popular skiing area in winter. Access along the B6277 is usually good in all but the hardest conditions as the road is kept open throughout the winter. It is the sole link into larger towns for the whole mass of villages in Upper Teesdale, and even the Alston area. The main skiing area is usually on Langdon Common where the even slopes of a dry gully on Three Pikes hill provide good conditions well into spring.

A glance at the OS map will show what intense activity went on here when mining lead was a profitable business. Hushing, to wash away the surface, was practised here as elsewhere in the dales and scarred gullies can still be seen after at least a century. A whole hotchpotch of field tracks criss-cross the area east of Langdon Beck, usually connecting smallholdings with mines higher on the fell side, the paths being the result of miners making their own routes home.*(1)

Two miles downstream from the confluence of Langdon Beck with the Tees the valley scenery changes dramatically from bleak, wild, open moorland at first to a wooded valley, but soon to gentle pastures below Newbiggin. The transition is dramatically marked by the thundering of **High Force**. Especially after a spate of

High Force
B6277, 5 miles north-west of Middleton-in-Teesdale. Easy access by footpath below High Force Hotel, small fee.

The Pennine Way passes close to Low Force.

heavy rain this magnificent fall is one of Britain's wonders – not the highest by a long way, but certainly one of the biggest in volume of water. In dry weather the fall occupies just one 70ft drop, but after rain another fall appears on the right of the dolerite buttress. This is a favourite vantage point and also one where people are caught unawares when a heavy rainfall in the Cross Fell area causes the river to rise in minutes. What was earlier a babbling rivulet can suddenly become an angry torrent. So watch for the signs and never climb onto the island if there is the chance of a storm around.

Most visitors to High Force approach it by way of a path through the grounds opposite High Force Hotel for which, of course, they have to pay. The view is worth every penny, but this way has a disadvantage. Apart from the small area of woodland around the falls, no further exploration is possible. A much more entertaining walk is to cross the Tees below Low Force at Wynch Bridge and walk upstream along the Pennine Way track.

**High Force Walk
4 miles – 2 hours**

The waterfalls of Teesdale rightly command their full complement of superlatives. All delight the eye of the visitor and it is not surprising to find one hidden in a side valley often missed and neglected other than by those who have discovered its charms. This is the small fall in the valley behind **Bowlees Visitor Centre** where

Bowlees Visitor Centre
B6277, 3 miles
north-west of
Middleton-in-Teesdale.

Causeway Syke tumbles over the small shaley outcrop of **Gibson's Cave**. The fall has cut back the shale so much that it is possible to stand behind a curtain of water and look out on the woodland scene through a fine tracery. The approach to this gem is by the path behind Bowlees Chapel – it will only take a few minutes to climb to the fall and the chances are that while High Force is crowded, you will have this one all to yourself. Causeway Syke Valley is an ideal picnic spot on a warm summer day. The old chapel at Bowlees houses a visitor and information centre devoted to the natural history of Teesdale, where grandparents can show youngsters how to use lead pencils and slates once mined near Cauldron Snout. The little garden outside the centre is planted with a selection of local wild flowers and moorland grasses.

A short fieldpath from Bowlees leads down to the tree-shaded river and to **Wynch Bridge** where the Tees cascades through the series of dolerite steps known as **Low Force**.* The land west of the Tees hereabouts is part of the Teesdale Nature Reserve and as a result is out of bounds to the walker with the exception of one or two long distance public rights-of-way. One of them, the path across **Holwick Fell**, was a drove road where cattle were slowly walked south on their way to market from the Scottish Highlands. Cattle no longer walk to market and **Holwick**, a resting place for drovers on the long trek south, no longer echoes to the lowing of massed beasts. The village is at the end of an unclassified road, three miles north-west of Middleton-in-Teesdale, a tiny group of stone cottages and farms fitting snugly beneath the whinstone crags of Holwick Scars. A short walk through Mill Beck Wood, to the south-east of Holwick, leads to a hidden rocky gorge and an attractive waterfall. Known as Fairy Dell, it is on private land, but permission is usually granted to anyone wishing to ramble or picnic there: enquire at the Strathmore Arms in Holwick.

Below Low Force the valley widens a little and meadows appear on either side of the river, meadows which in summer are a mass of wild flowers lasting until haymaking. The Pennine Way path follows the west bank all the way from Middleton-in-Teesdale and with a bit of careful arrangement of transport back, the whole length of the Pennine Way between Langdon Beck and Middleton can be walked by easy-to-follow and well signposted paths. It is eight miles of the most superb

Gibson's Cave
Bowlees.
Shallow water worn cave. Access by footpath and nature trail from Bowlees Visitor Centre.

The first Wynch Bridge was unique in being the earliest suspension bridge in Europe. It was first built in 1744 and rebuilt in 1828 to give miners living on the east side of the Tees access to the mining areas of the western fells. Probably it was the narrowness of the river at this point and firm rock on both sides which made the bridge builders site it just below Low Force. One thing is certain, the bridge makes an excellent vantage point to admire the spectacular rock formations upstream to Low Force and the tree-lined slopes on either side.

Mill Beck Wood short Walk ¼ mile – ½ hour

Above Middleton-in-Teesdale.

**High Force and Low Force Walk
8 miles – 4 hours**

Middleton-in-Teesdale
A small, purpose-built early 19th-century town added by the London Lead Company to an existing, much older village. Used by the company as one of their northern mining headquarters.

and scenic walking, taking in High Force and Low Force on the way. The walk can be done in either direction, but upstream is probably the best as you do not have to turn around to admire the falls.

Middleton-in-Teesdale grew in importance when the London Lead Company built an estate village around Masterman Place. Making it their local headquarters, they opened an office to control mining interests which were worked on both sides of Teesdale until 1905. The most striking feature of Middleton is its wide, grassy main street with the ornate cast-iron Bainbridge Memorial Fountain at one end. The present church is Victorian, probably built on Norman foundations. Town End Chapel to the east is a magnificent piece of Victorian architecture. **Stotley Hall** is about 1½ miles away, along the Barnard Castle road, an attractive example of a prosperous 17th-century farmhouse. Regular cattle auctions, quaint shops and coaching inns complete the rural scene of Middleton-in-Teesdale.*(1)

A short car ride along the narrow lane which climbs north out of Middleton around Hudeshope Beck to Coldberry Moor will take you past some of the old mines – do not go in them. Some fine examples of hushing can be found above the sharp bends on either side of the crossing of Hudeshope Beck. This is where the hillside has been washed away and traces of exposed ore-bearing rock can still be found.

The Pennine Way reaches Teesdale by cutting north-east across the corner of a long ridge running down from Lune Moor. Between the Pennine Way path and the B6276 Brough road through Lunedale, a conspicuous round hill with a plantation of trees on its summit can be seen. This is **Kirkcarrion** and is said to be haunted. How true the story is can only be guessed, but the mound has some ancient significance being the site of a massive tumulus.

Below Kirkcarrion is the **Lune Valley** – not the Lancashire River Lune but a much shorter stream and one which enters the Tees from the west. This river flows from the southerly end of the Cross Fell, Dufton Fell and Murton Fell range and in its upper reaches drains an area of wilderness uncrossed by any path and claimed by the military as a practice area. Traces of old mining activity can be found above 1,400ft. The valley's lower reaches have been dammed to make Selset and Grassholme reservoirs, both of which are stocked with fish. Apart from the Pennine Way path there is little to attract the walker into Lunedale, but the motor road B6276 from Middleton to Brough is a delightful high level motor route on a fine day.

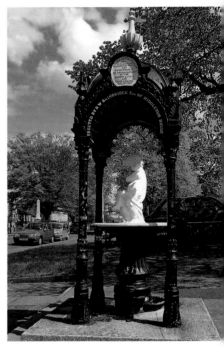

Memorial fountain, Middleton-in-Teesdale.

Downstream from where the Lune joins the Tees the valley bottom is flat and gradually widens with ever improving lush grazing, and so sets a pattern which is continued until industrial Teeside is reached. The line of stone cottages that are **Mickleton** occupy a sunny rise about a mile south of the confluence of the Lune and the Tees. Neolithic burials have been found nearby.

At the height of their fortunes the London Lead Company built a crushing mill at **Eggleston**. With this they attempted to extract the maximum amount of ore from mines higher up the main and side valleys. Eggleston, surrounded by a complex of 'B' roads to the east of the Tees, was more important in the past than it is today; since prehistoric times in fact. There was a

(1) It is hard to say exactly when lead mining ceased as a commercially viable enterprise in the Dales as some small scale mining went on intermittently until the 1920s, but it is generally reckoned that cheap imports of lead from America, Australia and Spain killed off the Dales' industry from the mid-1880s onwards. The Middleton area mines were about the last of the major sites to close.

Bowes Museum, Barnard Castle.

stone circle nearby, but regrettably it disappeared when the stones were broken up for road building. A drove road came south from Hexham through Eggleston and divided, one section going eastwards along the Tees while the other crossed Romaldkirk Moor to join the one south to Stainmore. The bridge across the Tees below Eggleston Hall was built in the 17th century, probably before then stock and people had to cross the river by a ford which could be hazardous when the river was in spate. There is also a delightful pack-horse bridge of similar date which crosses the village stream near the church. This church is Victorian and replaced one of earlier date; its ruins are in the private grounds of Eggleston Hall to the south. The hall is 19th-century and a fine example of a Victorian country gentleman's house.

The 12th-century church of St Rumwald, son of a king of Northumberland, is set at the end of a narrow alley which leads off the large village green. It is frequently referred to as 'Cathedral of the Dales', and was completed about 1290.

On the other side of Eggleston Bridge the road climbs gently to the beautifully situated village of **Romaldkirk**.* Houses built through the centuries add charm and character to the place. Southwards across Baldersdale which the water company is determined to drown (there are now three reservoirs), is **Cotherstone** once home of the Fitzhughs and where the castle has provided convenient building materials for the villagers from time to time; as witness several cottages which are made from worked stones of higher quality than would have normally been used. The Tees on either side of Barnard Castle is tree-lined and conveniently placed

Barnard Castle.

bridges north of Cotherstone make it possible to link up paths which follow both banks. **Lartington**, on the B6277 into Barnard Castle, shelters behind a wood and serves the needs of its hall and park built in the reign of Charles I. Lartington Hall is the venue for the annual Teesdale Country Fair.

The first time visitor to **Barnard Castle**, on approaching the town from the south-east, may think they have been transported to France. This misunderstanding can be excused because the massive building which stands on rising ground east of the town and resembles a French château was in fact designed by a French architect, Jules Pellachet. The **Bowes Museum** was originally built for George Bowes, illegitimate son of the tenth Earl of Strathmore and from whom he inherited vast Durham estates and collieries. The foundation stone was laid in 1869 but George Bowes and his wife with whom he shared the idea of a vast museum of antiquities and art, died before it was completed in 1892. Over the years the building became something of a white elephant until it was taken over by Durham County Council in 1952. It is now run efficiently as the

Barnard Castle
A67 Darlington to Bowes road.
Barnard Castle Town
Covered market cross and Blagroves House of particular interest.
Bowes Museum
Outskirts of Barnard Castle on the Whorlton road. French-style château housing a collection of national importance including paintings by El Greco and Goya.

Bowes Castle
On A66, 4 miles south-west of Barnard Castle. Massive 12th-century stone keep overlooking the River Greta. Admission free.

county museum covering diverse subjects from local Roman relics to the great masters and is regarded as having one of the finest art collections outside London. Galleries are devoted to period French furniture. Pride of place in the main entrance is given to a life size working model of a silver swan which catches tiny fishes! The museum and surrounding gardens are open all year except Christmas and New Year.

Barnard Castle is a venerable town full of delightfully interesting corners. Its castle was built to command an important river crossing and is named after Barnard (Bernard) son of Guy Balliol who was granted land here by William II in 1093. The river crossing on this important north-south route is still marked by a venerable bridge dating from 1569. The castle was extended and strengthened several times over the years and at one time was the property of Warwick the Kingmaker through whom it passed to Richard III. It is his emblem, the wild boar, which can be seen on the wall of the Great Chamber. The castle is now maintained by English Heritage and opens at their standard advertised times.

The ancient street names of Barnard Castle speak of the time when the town was a secure place against Scottish raiders and it was safer to live near a castle for protection. Streets with names like Newgate, Bridgegate and Thorngate radiate from the castle. Thorngate, lined for part of its length by 18th-century town houses, descends to the river past an old mill and then leads on to The Bank. Above it all stands the solidly built octagonal market cross which dominated local trade when the only source of fresh meat and vegetables was that brought in from outside farms. Built in 1747, the colonnaded shelter is crowned by a cupola and weathervane. The town hall, lit by elegant Venetian windows, fills the upper storey. Further down the street, 16th century Blagroves House, now a restaurant, is three storeys high beneath a gabled roof.*

Charles Dickens stayed at the King's Head Hotel in Horsemarket when he was collecting material for Nicholas Nickleby. In Newgate a plaque marks the site of a shop owned by the man who was the inspiration for Dicken's Master Humphrey's Clock, intended as a frame for both Barnaby Rudge and The Old Curiosity Shop.

Egglestone Abbey
1 mile south of Barnard Castle on the Whorlton road. Ruins of small abbey, 13th to-14th- century nave survives.

From Barnard Castle a field path leads downstream through East Lendings to a view of the most northerly of the Dales' abbeys, **Egglestone Abbey.** Founded in the 12th century by Premonstratensian canons, this elegant abbey is the very epitome of holiness as it sits in quiet splendour above the tree-lined Tees. After the Dissolution part of the abbey was converted into a farmhouse and several additions were made in later years, especially in the 17th century. Much of the cruciform, aisleless church still survives, especially the nave and chancel. The windows are early English although the matching east window is thought to be 17th-century. Beautifully carved medieval grave slabs dot the green outside.

The octagonal market cross in Barnard Castle.

Downstream again a path follows the course of the river into **Rokeby Park** and its hall (open to the public). **Rokeby Hall** was built in the Palladian style in 1735 by Sir Thomas Robinson, at one time Governor of Barbados, and he was known locally as 'Long Sir Tom' from his build and angular gait. Rokeby is the true home of Velazquez's *Rokeby Venus* which now hangs in the National Gallery in London, but many other paintings and a unique collection of needlework by Anne Marritt (1726-97) are on display in the compact main buildings. On the eastern edge of the park is Mortham Tower, a 14th-century pele tower, the fortified home of the Rokeby family for generations until it was bought by Sir Thomas Robinson who altered and extended the wings which had been added in Tudor times.

The river separating Rokeby Park from Mortham Tower is the Greta. Water flowing along it has drained from the wilds of Stainmore across which runs the A66, an important trans-Pennine highway since Roman times. A drove road south crossed the Greta to the west on a natural limestone bridge known as **God's Bridge**,

God's Bridge (NY957 127), ¼ mile south of Pasture End Farm, 2 miles west of Bowes on A66.

and from there the route wandered south into Swaledale. Rokeby Park is bounded by the A66(T) which still follows the line of the Roman road to this day. The road by Rokeby takes a sharp swing to the south-east away from the Tees and aims for the A1 at Scotch Corner. Hard by Greta Bridge are the earth bank remains of a fort and beyond is one of the best features of the southern part of Teesdale - the wooded ravine of **Brignall Banks**, through which the Greta flows its last few miles before joining the main river. Here is another of those delightful walks where you can be certain of being able to wander quietly and hardly see another soul all day.

Whorlton, 4 miles downstream of Barnard Castle, is a picturesque grouping of terraced cottages and attractive gardens on the north bank of the Tees. A steep road descends to a suspension bridge (built in 1829) and nearby on the south bank is a riverside lido and picnic site.*

The romantic ruin of St Mary's Church, above the eastern side of the valley, is over a quarter of a mile from Brignall village and one cannot but puzzle over why it was built there rather than in the village. No doubt people tired of walking through damp woodland to and from church and in 1833 they built one in a more convenient place, although burials continued in the old churchyard for another 50 years.

Just under 2 miles south of the A66 and in a wild and desolate spot on Scargill Moor stands the site of a series of Roman shrines. The site is about a mile west-north-west of Spanham Farm (NZ016101) and towards Eller Beck; the altar stones are in Bowes Museum.

Bowes is a quieter place now that the A66 by-passes it to the north on an embankment. It has stood here since the Romans built their fort of *Lavatræ* to command the approaches to Stainmore. Likewise, the Normans following the Conquest built a castle here in 1171, but it was never more than a fortified tower. Little remains of *Lavatræ*, most of the stones having been used to build the castle and later the village church, but the ditches and some of the ramparts of *Lavatræ* can be seen. The fort covered an area of about three acres and from excavations it appears that it was occupied from the second to fourth centuries AD. Water for the fort was brought by aqueduct from Levy (or Laver) Pool about two miles away to the north. *Lavatræ* was strategically sited at the junction of two roads, one running north-east to *Vinovia* (Binchester) to join Dere Street on its way north to Hadrian's Wall. The other road runs south-east for 25 miles to *Cataractonium* (modern Catterick), a garrison town even to this day.

On the edge of Bowes is Dotheboys Hall, featured in Charles Dickens' *Nicholas Nickleby*. Dotheboys Hall was

Vintage cars pause outside England's highest inn at Tan Hill.

a private school run by the sadistic and greedy Wackford Squeers who thought nothing of starving and beating his charges and whose education was his least thought. The character of Wackford Squeers was built on a real person who unfortunately was typical of his time before legislation came about following protests from such radical thinkers as Dickens.

An arm of the Pennine Way passes through Bowes before moving north again to Baldersdale. The Greta flows roughly parallel to the A66 and at one time was followed by a railway line, one of the most difficult lines in the country.*

The main Pennine Way route follows Sleightholme Beck all the way from England's highest pub, the **Tan Hill Inn**. This pub has served well throughout the years, helping travellers of all kinds from gypsies and cattle drovers to Pennine Way walkers, and more importantly the miners who dug coal from shallow pits which still dot the moorland with their open and unfenced shafts. The annual show of the Swaledale Sheep-breeders Association is held at Tan Hill on the last Thursday in May.

Signposted from the west-bound carriageway of the A66(T) across Stainmore, a branch of the **Otter Trust** at Vale House rehabilitates orphaned otter cubs and others in 230 acres of upland farm land. Visitors are welcome daily from late May to the end of October.

*Trains travelling on the steep west to east gradient had to have an extra engine and the story is that, contrary to the rules which demanded that the train be stopped for an extra engine to be coupled, to save time the second locomotive would chase the train, and without being coupled would push from the rear; dangerous but effective.

Otter Trust
Vale House Farm near Bowes.

Swaledale

The cairns of Nine Standards Rigg.

Narrow, sinuous and always grand, Swaledale is the most northerly of Yorkshire's major dales. Its river, the Swale, is born among peat hags and heather at 2,000ft on Birkdale Common, near the boundary with Cumbria.

For its first few miles it is a frisky moorland beck, becoming youthfully exuberant above Keld, lively and increasingly mature in the next 10 miles to Reeth, and never losing its unique Pennine character until it leaves Richmond behind and enters the Vale of York. The enclosing fells of Upper Swaledale are mostly acid moorland on sandstones and shales. Plant life is limited, grazing meagre. Down stream, limestone outcrops as crags and scars around Keld mingle with alluvial soils in the valleys to support a richer flora. Stock find good pasture on hillsides and in valley meadows where lush grasses ripen in summer.

Gunnerside was first settled by Norsemen.

*Utterly functional, and placed exactly where they were needed, the stone barns were for storing hay in the upper storey, and housing cattle below, usually from November to May. An average barn would store hay gathered from one or two fields, and accommodate four cattle, a small centre for foddering, milking and 'mucking-out' during the long winter months.

All buildings are made of stone – farms, barns, villages. These, together with the enclosing dry-stone walls built patiently by craftsmen of yesteryear, developed much of the character of the dale. Above Reeth, Swaledale was very much an area of Norse settlement. Until the early 1900's some Dales' farmers practised a method of husbandry still common in parts of Norway and the Alps. A subsidiary house further up the dale was occupied during the summer, with sheep and cattle grazing pastures on the high fells, while valley fields produced the hay essential for winter feed.

It was for this hay that barns, or laithes were built. Nowhere in Britain is the pattern of dispersed barns shown so well as in Swaledale. The area of high Dales' pasture west of Gunnerside is a fine example of this still practised method of farming husbandry.* With changing methods of farming, some Dales' barns have become redundant and in order to preserve their unique character, many are being put to other uses such as Camping Barns.

Swaledale experienced relative prosperity during the height of the lead mining industry. Men of Swaledale were renowned for their skills below ground, skills which were developed long before the Roman occupation, and continued into the present century. Not only

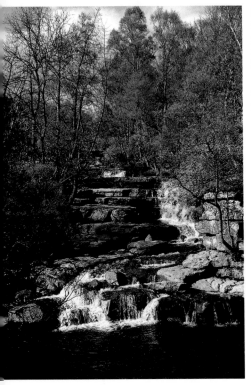

Ease Gill below Keld.

did they mine lead but a little silver was found, though never enough to be commercially viable. Coal was also mined extensively beneath the moors around Tan Hill, providing fuel not only for domestic use, but mostly for lead smelting. Ownership of the lead mines had a long and complex history since the days when the Romans used it for waterpipes and roof cover. Monasteries owning vast areas of the North until the Dissolution were keen to exploit the underground riches to help cover the huge roof areas of their churches. Northern lead was used on cathedrals all over the country and a thriving trade started in medieval times transporting pigs (or ingots) of lead.

The highest village in the dale is Keld and it separates two faces of Swaledale. To the west the uplands are bleak and boggy, but eastwards the narrow valley is a delight, with its villages spaced almost equidistantly down the dale. These villages still serve as focal points for the hardy hill farms with their land on the steep valley sides, and common grazing on the open moors. In spring the moors are alive with the cry of the curlew, a call evocative of the vast open spaces of the High Pennines, together with the sound of wind soughing through the coarse grasses of the fells.

Coast to Coast walkers enter Swaledale by way of the enigmatic line of tall stone cairns known as Nine Standards Rigg.

A multitude of small streams which drain Mallerstang Edge flow through the soggy mass of Birkdale Common and join west of Keld to form the River Swale proper. Pennine Wayfarers and Coast-to-Coast walkers use Keld as a stopping place. **Keld**, which means a 'place by the river' was first settled by the Norsemen but the village today owes much of its appearance to the lead mining days of the last century. The dour village, still echoing its non-conformist traditions, huddles around a tiny square, away from the lonely road from Swaledale to Kirkby Stephen. Scattered relics of a now dead lead industry dot the nearby fells; ruined Crackpot Hall above wooded Swinnergill is the result of mining too close beneath it.

Not only does the Pennine Way pass through Keld, it also marks the half-way point on the Coast to Coast Long Distance Walk. Designed by the late A. Wainwright, the route from St Bees Head in Cumbria to Robin Hood's Bay on the north-east coast enters the realms of this guide at Kirkby Stephen. It then climbs to the enigmatic line of ancient cairns on Nine Standards Rigg, where the path drops down to the hospitality of Keld. Beyond Keld the walk winds its way through abandoned lead mining areas along the northern side of Swaledale as far as Richmond. Here it crosses the Vale of Mowbray to reach the escarpment of the North York Moors and eventually the North Sea.

An ancient track, known as The Corpse Way, from the days when Swaledale's only church was over 10 miles away at Grinton, runs east across the airy side of Kisdon Hill from Keld. Still recognisable for much of its length it can be followed by valley road and foothpath along the dale.

The Pennine Way passes through Keld, a favourite half-way stop for 'Coast to Coast' walkers.

A house in the village of Keld.

The stone houses of Thwaite.

Kisdon Force
1/2 mile east of Keld on B6270.
Waterfall, approached by an easy footpath from Keld.

Thwaite
At junction of Hawes and B6270 roads, in Upper Swaledale.
Typical Dales' village of Norse origin.

As though to recompense for the bleak heights in the upper limits of the dale, the river scenery around Keld is a delight. Here the Swale has cut through to the hard limestone beds which appear in dramatic steps, creating lively waterfalls. Of these, **Kisdon Force** is the best, set in a deep wooded gorge below Kisdon Hill. The hill separates the river's course from that of the road between Keld and Thwaite.

Thwaite is a little huddle of stone houses and farms which seem to crouch together in mutual protection against winter storms. Here again is a village founded by Norsemen, for Thwaite means 'a clearing in woodland'. There are not many trees now, but if the valley below Keld is anything to go by then this sheltered part of the dale would once have been densely wooded. The trees were felled to create farmland and never given the opportunity to regenerate.

Swaledale's most famous sons of modern times were Richard and Cherry Kearton who were born at Thwaite and went to school in Muker, the next village down the dale. A lintel decorated with wildlife indicates the house where they were born and their names live on at the friendly Kearton Guest House in Thwaite. Towards the end of the last century these two did more than anyone to popularise natural history when the subject was considered to be far too academic for the masses.

High up on the eastern side of Shunner Fell and almost at the summit of the Thwaite-Hawes road are the **Buttertubs**, a series of shallow potholes easily accessible from the road. They are deep enough to break the bones of anyone foolish enough to wander carelessly on their brink and fall, but shallow enough to see the shade-loving harts-tongue and other ferns which live in them. The technical term for the Buttertubs is 'swallow hole' and perhaps this is an apt description of them as they have been formed by the action of water dissolving parts of the limestone strata. Frost action, followed by more water, has created what is seen today.

Muker, meaning 'a cultivated enclosure', is another Norse settlement, but built on earlier foundations, as indicated by the number of Neolithic artefacts which have been unearthed from time to time around the village. The church is 16th-century and corpses were brought to its burial ground from most of the upper dale. Prior to 1580 when it was built, all burials were at Grinton. Most of the original character of Muker Church was lost by 18th and 19th-century alterations, but it did not lose any of its charm and is still the focal point of the village.

The Buttertubs – a series of shallow potholes at the side of the Hawes-Thwaite road.

Buttertubs
2¹/₂ miles south of Thwaite on Hawes road, below top of the pass. Shallow potholes on hillside on both sides of the road.

Above and below: the charming village of Muker.

Muker is especially proud of its band which was formed in 1879. Brass bands seem to have been a feature of the old lead mining villages and were encouraged by the lead companies, especially the London Lead Company who set their employees' welfare high on their priorities.

Downstream from Muker short tributary valleys branch off at almost regular intervals north and south. Some are traversed by roads, others by paths, but all are of interest and worth exploring. This is where the true unspoilt character of the Dales is still to be found. **Oxnop Ghyll**, entering Swaledale from the south below the Askrigg road, is such a valley, a ghyll dale where mountain ash, scrub birch, hawthorn, holly and willow fill the sheltered ravine echoing a time before man began to dominate the landscape. The wood was a favourite hunting ground for the Keartons in their search for wildlife subjects. A path skirts the boundary of the woodland and starts from the roadside close to the junction of the B6270, valley road and the side lane to Gunnerside.

Opposite Oxnop Ghyll and Kearton's Wood, the Swale is spanned by **Ivelet Bridge**, an excellent example of a pack-horse bridge which carried an ancient track across to **Gunnerside** village. This name again comes from old Norse and means 'Gunner's Pasture'. Above the village to the north **Old Gang mines** were one of the most famous of the lead mining complexes in the Dales.

Gunnerside is at the foot of Gunnerside Gill which rises beneath Rogan's Seat about six miles away. Gunnerside Gill is a living museum of lead mining and two moorland tracks which follow its edges served the complex, almost self-supporting, industry. The valley sides are scarred with the results of repeated hushings which have left alluvial fans of debris at the foot of the slope. Two smelt mills, Lownathwaite and Blakethwaite, were worked well into the late 19th century. Spoil heaps and the remains of various buildings associated with mining activity can readily be seen.

There is an excellent traverse of the top of Gunnerside Gill's ravine. This walk which starts from Gunnerside village and visits many of the ruined mine buildings, spoil heaps and hushes, is covered by an informative trail leaflet produced by the Yorkshire Dales National Park Authority.

Ivelet Bridge.

Gunnerside Gill Walk
8 miles – 4 hours

The bleak remains of the Old Gang lead mill.

A high level path joins Gunnerside to Low Row and Feetham linking villages further down the dale which have almost merged, but which still keep their individual character. Thomas Armstrong, the Yorkshire novelist, lived hereabouts and his book, *Adam Brunskill,* is based on lead mining in this part of Swaledale during the second half of last century.

Hazel Brow Farm at Low Row offers a unique opportunity to find out about life on a real working Dales' farm. Visitors are especially welcome during lambing time (March to April).

Healaugh, at the foot of Barney Beck, was originally a Saxon dwelling place in a forest clearing. The village serves as a suitable base for exploring the upper reaches of Barney Beck, in the area known as Hard Level Gill. This is where the remains of one of the most famous and productive mining complexes can be seen. Known as the Old Gang mining field, it is possible to get within a mile or so of it by a car parked near Surrender Bridge on the moorland road north from Feetham to Arkengarthdale. Here a beck-side track leads upstream to the mining complex below the dale head. Even though all is now ruins, it is easy to pick out the various buildings from the foundations. The mines were owned by a variety of persons and companies through more than 150 years. Lead ore dug out of the Old Gang mines was processed entirely within the confines of Hard Level Gill before being carried out of the dale by pack-horse trains.

Do not attempt to enter any of the old mines – they are all in dangerous condition.

One of the attractive qualities of Upper Swaledale is its ability to allow the pedestrian to walk almost all the way from Keld to Grinton by riverside footpaths. Except where the road touches the river bank, a public foot-path exists all the way down the valley. From Keld to Muker paths exist on both sides of the south-flowing river, but from Muker onwards the path keeps mainly to the north bank.

Early man left his mark with a giant earthwork at **Maiden Castle** and its attendant tumuli and dykes high on the fell side opposite Healaugh and Reeth. Theories abound, but no real answer can be offered about its original purpose. Reached by footpaths west of Grinton, one can only stand in awe at the tremendous labours involved in such huge earth moving schemes.

An impression of Swaledale life in the heyday of lead mining is displayed in the Swaledale Folk Museum at

The village green, Reeth.

Langthwaite in
Arkengarthdale.

Reeth
A once important lead
mining centre. Attractive
houses and inns
surround a pleasant
village green. Swaledale
Folk Museum at Reeth
Green depicts life in
Swaledale in bygone
days, including lead
mining, farming, and
village life.

Arkengarthdale
Above Reeth on B6270
Remains of mining
activity with ruined
smelt mills, flues,
hushes, powder house.
Pleasant short walks
take in most of these
features.

Reeth. The museum not only covers the history of lead mining in the locality, but also highlights social conditions of bygone days from the point of view of a farming community as well as mining.

In Saxon times **Reeth** was only a settlement on the forest edge but by the time of the Norman Conquest it had grown sufficiently in importance to be noted in the *Domesday Book*. Later it became a centre for hand-knitting and the local lead industry was controlled from here, but it was always a market town for the local farming community. Its 18th-century houses and hotels clustered around the triangular village green make it one of the honeypots of the Dales. Down the ages, Reeth has been a bustling place, in the middle of the 19th century there were seven fairs and a weekly market. Now the streets around the green can be packed with cars on a fine summer day. In early autumn an annual show and sheep sales are held on the meadows below the town.

Reeth fills a sheltered position above the meeting of Arkle Beck and the Swale. **Arkengarthdale**, the side dale climbing north-west from Reeth, had one of the first turnpike roads to be built in the area. It was originally part of a drove road which came south from Teesdale to Tan Hill then down Arkengarthdale as far as Langthwaite before climbing over Reeth Moor to Feetham. From there the drove road continued south to Askrigg in Wensleydale and by way of the Roman road across Cam Fell into

Ribblesdale. The reason for improving the Arkengarthdale section of the drove road in 1741 was to help move coal mined around Tan Hill down to the lower part of the dale. Here it was used to fuel smelting furnaces around Langthwaite.

If there is one dale where the whole story of lead mining can be seen from mine to smelt mill then Arkengarthdale is it. The museum at Reeth tells everything in graphic form, but the true museum is to be found above the dale. Hushes scar the hillsides; levels where mines were driven either horizontally or at an angle from the middle slopes. Deep shafts open dangerously on the upper fells, and ruined crushing mills and smelting mills dot the valley floor. All this was activity fuelled by the coal of Tan Hill. Most of the mines were owned by Charles Bathurst and his descendants who operated as the CB Company. The only surviving roofed building from this complex is the powder house in a field by the road junction west of the CB Hotel, dating from about 1807.

The townships of Arkengarthdale were founded before mining came to dominate the dale. **Arkle Town** was a Norse settlement which gave its name to the dale, but the main village is **Langthwaite**, whose church, however, is one of the Commissioners' churches built soon after Waterloo. Above it is the delightful Georgian-styled CB Hotel.*

In a side valley and reached by a side road from Langthwaite, is the hamlet of **Booze**. There is no pub, and the name means 'the house by the curve' – there are no connections with inns or drunkenness!

There are old miners' tracks on both sides of the upper valley which will give the walker ample scope especially when used to explore the mining remains, but the road from Reeth to Tan Hill is probably the best way of exploring Arkengarthdale.

Rich deposits of lead were worked on the opposite side of the Swale from Arkengarthdale. These are mostly centred on a broad swathe above Grinton where the inevitable scars left by hushing and other mining debris cover the fell sides. In early times **Grinton** was the centre of Swaledale, with the only consecrated ground in the dale. Corpses brought to it from the upper dale were carried in wicker baskets by relays of men from each village through which it passed. The

*Devotees of the TV programme about a Dales' vet's life, All Creatures Great and Small, will instantly recognise the hump-backed bridge and attractive group of cottages just off the main road at Langthwaite. For many episodes the bridge was used in the opening scene. The watersplash, used in another series, is not far away on the moorland road to Feetham.

Grinton
Church is often claimed to be the 'Cathedral of the Dales'.

Grinton once had the only graveyard in Upper Swaledale.

custom continued until 1586 when the Muker burial ground was consecrated. Grinton Church, which has often been referred to as the 'Cathedral of the Dales', was originally Norman but was added to in the 13th and 14th centuries. Of its many interesting features, perhaps the best is the 'Leper's Squint' where people with this dreadful affliction were able to watch the service without actually coming into contact with the rest of the congregation. The village inn sits at the junction of the valley road with the one over to Wensleydale, and a turreted shooting lodge on the moors above Grinton now serves as a very well appointed Youth Hostel.

Man has lived a long time around Grinton. The many tumuli and earthworks surrounding the village indicate a great involvement with some force either political or religious, but none have had as much effort put into them as the huge and complex earthwork which appears to have been a barrier between Grinton Gill and the enigmatic earthwork of Maiden Castle. Roman remains found hereabouts give rise to the thought of battles between the invaders and local tribes.

On **Cogden Moor** above Grinton, and just off the Leyburn road stands the remains of a smelt mill built by the London Lead Company in about 1840. After recent conservation it is one of the best examples in the Dales. The easiest way to reach these interesting ruins is by a path which follows the course of Cogden Beck from the sharp hairpin bend half a mile above Grinton Lodge. The whole of this valley is scarred with the remains of hushing and an hour or so may be spent picking over the stones to find samples of lead ore, fluorspar and other minerals. From the mill continue onto the moor to an area of spoil heaps before swinging round to the left to rejoin the road beyond the old Wellington Vein Mine.

After all the wanderings in and around Swaledale's mining past a complete change of environment comes with the south-west facing villages of Fremington and Marrick on the north side of the dale below Reeth. Their history is almost as old as man in the dale. Below **Marrick**, and reached by a long flight of steps, is **Marrick Priory** a 12th-century Benedictine nunnery, whose chapel is now used as a Field Study Centre. Further downstream is Ellerton Abbey, founded by the nuns of the Cistercian order in the 14th century. Little remains of this nunnery except a tower and parts of the nave walls.

The main road from Grinton (the B6270) accompanies the river to Richmond with good valley scenery all the way. In contrast, the old road to Richmond which climbs high above Marrick has more open views to offer of these lower reaches of the Pennine section of Swaledale.

Marrick Priory.

Marrick Priory
Reached by a stone causeway from Marrick village, $^1/_2$ mile to the north-east.

Marske-in-Swaledale, although strictly in the side dale of Marske Beck, is idyllic, purely agricultural and surrounded by wooded hills beneath wild moors. The hall was home and birthplace of the Hutton family who provided two Archbishops of York, one of whom, Matthew, became Archbishop of Canterbury in 1757. Marske's church has Norman origins, with additions in the 13th and 17th centuries.

On a high rocky crag above the Swale stands a memorial stone erected in 1606 by Robert Willance. It commemorates his survival after his horse fell from the crag in fog. Willance broke a leg and only saved himself by cutting open the dead horse's belly and thrusting his leg inside to keep it warm. The old road descends to Richmond, past Beacon Hill which, on a clear day, is an excellent view point and from which the spires of York Minster can be seen far to the south.

Swaledale's capital, **Richmond** with its cobbled ways and attractive town houses, is the northern gateway to the Dales. The castle commanded all access in and out of

Swaledale and was manned by troops whose 20th-century counterparts train at nearby Catterick. Earl Alan Rufus built his massive castle soon after the Norman Conquest and roofed it with Swaledale lead. Later the upkeep of the town walls was paid for by lead coming out of the dale, on a toll of two old pence a mule load. Richmond became a stronghold in an area often under attack by Scottish invaders. Fragments of the old walls can still be seen in Friar's Wynd and at the bar on Cornforth Hill.*

The cobbled streets and church of Richmond.

Richmond
Ancient market town and guardian of the northern dales. Castle was built in 1071 by Alan Rufus for William the Conqueror to quell the rebellious North. The 11th-century remains of the curtain wall and domestic buildings are combined with the 100ft high keep and its hugely thick walls, which was added in the 12th century.

Legends link Richmond Castle with King Arthur and his Knights of the Round Table; a local worthy is reputed to have stumbled upon their treasure in a hidden cavern beneath the castle, but fled on seeing the assembled warriors. Unfortunately he could not find the cave again so King Arthur and his Knights still sleep awaiting the call in England's hour of need.

As Richmond grew in importance it became the focal point for the commercial and agricultural interests of the dale and also the surrounding area; there has been a market since 1155. The town incidentally is far older than its Surrey namesake. Tradesmen settled in the town and formed their guilds, some of which have existed in Richmond for over 400 years. Nowadays the guilds are only interesting anachronisms which meet twice yearly for dinners, their only function to appoint a new 'freeman' to their numbers. At one time the office of freeman carried a number of useful privileges, not the least being the freedom from road, bridge and market tolls anywhere in England!

Richmond Castle, an English Heritage protected property, dominates the town centre. There are magnificent views of Swaledale from the top of the keep. General Robert Baden Powell, founder of the scouting movement, commanded the castle from 1908 to 1910. During both World Wars conscientious objectors were imprisoned in the castle cells; not open to the public at the time of compiling this guide.

The local regiment is the Green Howards who, along with the Royal Corps of Signals and RAF Catterick, can march through Richmond with bands playing and bayonets fixed. The Green Howards Regimental Museum is housed in Trinity Church Square opposite the Kings Head. The *Lass of Richmond Hill*, Frances l'Anson, lived at Hill House and was immortalised by Leonard McNally who wrote the song and married her in 1787. Richmond is home to the fine Georgian Theatre Royal close to the market place, built in 1788 by Samuel Butler and faithfully restored in 1963 by a local society. The theatre with its tiny authentic Georgian stage, to which one must add the crowded Georgian intimacy of its auditorium, gives a varied repertoire of plays and concerts throughout the season.

Reached by road or by a short riverside path through woods below Richmond is **Easby Abbey**. This Premonstratensian abbey was founded in 1152 by Roaldus, Constable of Richmond. When Henry VIII was carrying out his Dissolution of the Monasteries the canons supported the Pilgrimage of Grace. Joining other northern religious houses in 1596, they started out for London to petition the King. On the King's orders the Duke of Norfolk attacked the protestors at Skipworth Moor, and many of those captured were later executed on Tower Hill.

Beyond Richmond the Swale meanders on through rich agricultural land of the northern part of the Vale of York, before joining the Ure on its way to York, and eventually into the Humber and the North Sea.

Richmond Castle dominates the town centre. Its keep is one of the tallest in England.

Green Howards Regimental Museum Trinity Church Square on Victoria Road.

Wensleydale

In sharp contrast to its northerly sisters, Wensleydale shows a more gentle face even in its upper reaches. Where Swaledale is narrow, Wensleydale soon broadens into lush pasture. Its mining activity was confined to working an extension of the Grinton ores, and through the centuries Wensleydale evolved a distinctive pastoral character which makes it a particular favourite for many visitors.

The name Wensleydale derives not from a river but from a village. Indeed, were it called by its ancient river name the valley should really be Yoredale, but today the river is known as the Ure, which rises among the lonely mosses and sedge-grasses of Abbotside Common, on the eastern edge of Mallerstang.

Semer Water.

Burtersett in Wensleydale where Norsemen pastured their cattle each summer.

The river Ure's furthest point starts south of Hell Gill Bridge, close to the county boundaries of Cumbria and North Yorkshire, a line also used by the National Park. After a short southwards flow its waters, quickly augmented by other becks draining from the high fells, swing eastwards by the Moorcock Inn near Garsdale Head, and continue in this direction out beyond Leyburn and Jervaulx Abbey, where the flat lands of the Vale of York draw it southwards towards the Ouse.

Wensley village, several miles down the dale, was, during the 13th century, the only market in the valley and it is perhaps this medieval importance which led to its giving the valley the name by which it is now known. Today, Leyburn, near Wensley, and Hawes, in the upper dale, are the market towns, busy centres both agriculturally and as focal points for an increasing number of visitors.

Several of the river's high tributaries, notably from Widdale near Hawes, together with its tributary Snaizeholme Beck, contribute a greater volume of water, but a logical continuation upstream from the main dale leads to Garsdale Common where the Moorcock Inn at 1,063ft above sea level stands on the watershed.

Wensleydale

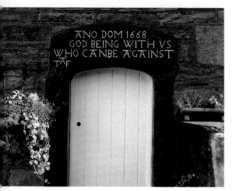

ANO DOM 1668
GOD BEING WITH VS
WHO CANBE AGAINST
TAF

A reflection of the times, lintel over the door of Crockett's Hotel, Hawes.

Side valleys are an important feature of Wensleydale, each in itself worthy of separate exploration. Widdale has been mentioned and with the exception of Apedale near Castle Bolton, all the central tributaries flow north into Wensleydale. Sleddale has a short run through Hawes, next comes Raydale with mysterious Semer Water, one of the Dale's few lakes, then Bishopdale with its own tributary of Walden Beck, Coverdale where they breed champion racehorses, and finally Colsterdale which joins the Ure near Masham and is probably the least known of all the minor dales.

Lady Anne Clifford came this way when she visited her northern estates. Many ancient footpaths and bridleways link Wensleydale to dales north and south. It is possible to walk the length of Wensleydale from the Moorcock Inn to Middleham using public footpaths and quiet side roads.

Appersett, at the mouth of Widdale and the first village in Upper Swaledale, is one of a group of hamlets near Hawes whose name includes a legacy from the days of Norse settlement and farming. A 'sett', or sætr, was a place for the summer pasturing of stock. Other examples further down the dale, are Burtersett, Countersett and Marsett.

Snaizeholme Beck Walk
4 miles – 2 hours

Widdale links across to Ribblesdale and forms a natural route for the B6255, with Widdale Fell to the north-west and Cam Pasture and Dodd Fell to the south and east. Widdale has its own tributary, Snaizeholme, and although there is no footpath out of the dale head, it is possible to follow Snaizeholme Beck all the way from the B6255 to Stone Gill Foot by right-of-way.

The Pennine Way passes through Hawes using a complex system of ancient roads and tracks on its route from Ribblesdale. This is part drove road and part Roman road across Cam Pasture and then a long sweeping run down from Dodd Fell by way of Sleddale Pasture on a delightful green road. It is these green roads which feature so much in the Pennine Dales of Yorkshire. They are often walled for most of their length and are therefore safe and easy to follow, stretching for mile after mile in solitude over the high fells of the Pennines. Invariably they follow the high ground over the shortest route between centres of agricultural population. Modern transport tends to shun their more exposed passage and has left the green roads alone.

Hawes has rightly been called 'the capital of Upper Wensleydale'. Its name comes from the Anglo-Saxon *haus*, meaning a mountain pass (such as Honister Hause in the Lake District, a major pass between Borrowdale and the Buttermere valley). Hawes is one of the highest market towns in England. Having held a market charter only since 1700, Hawes is a comparative newcomer but today it is a thriving little place linked by good roads to neighbouring dales, all easily accessible from the A684. Its growth increased when the railway came through the dale in 1878 and made it possible for Victorian tourists to 'discover' Upper Wensleydale. Since the decline of branch lines and the closure of what was scenically a most attractive railway, Hawes Station has been put to use as an information centre and also houses the Dales Countryside Museum where a comprehensive display of farm implements and mementoes of life in the Dales is on view. The bulk of the collection was made by two women who did much to record the past in these parts, Marie Hartley and Joan Ingilby. Industry in Hawes, apart from farming, has been specialised. At one time it was an important centre for hand-knitted hosiery and for 200 years has been noted for rope making. Hawes Ropeworks has become a popular tourist attraction where you can watch the production and maybe buy from a wide range of rope articles, including tethers for cows and horses.

Hawes is very busy during the tourist season with a weekly livestock market ,at its most active during sheep and lamb sales from August to October, at the east end of the town. Each year over 100,000 sheep and lambs change hands, together with over 12,000 head of cattle. Although Hawes' roots go back to the 15th century, few very old buildings remain; 17th-century dates and initials indicate their first owners. Walkers following the Pennine Way reach

Hawes is one of the highest market towns in England.

Hawes
Dales Countryside Museum, Station Yard Exhibits of life on Dales' farms.

Yorkshire Flowerpots Rural Workshops, Hawes. Wide range of terracotta garden ware made on the premises.

W. R. Outhwaite & Son, Ropemakers, Station Yard, Hawes. Traditional ropemaking from bell ropes to clothes lines.

Yorkshire Dales National Park Information Centre Station Yard, Hawes. Provides details of current events in the area, along with displays to help understand the environment of the National Park.

Hardraw Force.

**Great Shunner Fell Walk
12 miles – 6 hours**

Hardraw Force
1 mile north of Hawes.
Behind the Green
Dragon Inn, Hardraw.
Highest above-ground
waterfall in England.

**Wensleydale Creamery
Visitor centre.**

Hawes along a quaint stone flagged passage which enters the main street beneath an often flower decked archway.

Adjacent to and dominated by Hawes, the hamlet of **Gayle** is a much older place and is thought to be built on the foundations of a Celtic settlement. Visitors to Gayle will be difficult to please if they are not entranced by the gentle hypnotism of the series of waterfalls where Duerley Beck crosses the limestone beds and ledges above the bridge. Gayle Force is immediately above the bridge and Aysgill Force, some 30ft high, can be reached by a footpath to the south-west of the village. Wensleydale cheese, once produced from ewes' milk in farmhouses throughout the dale, is now made in the Hawes Creamery between Hawes and Gayle. The **Wensleydale Creamery** Visitor Centre explains how this famous cheese is made.

Pennine Way walkers leave Hawes by the Muker road and once over the river turn left to Hardraw where the Green Dragon Inn extracts a small toll to view the spectacle of **Hardraw Force** – England's highest above-ground waterfall (Gaping Gill and other pothole falls are greater, but below ground). At Hardraw, the soft Yoredale shales have been worn back by the force of water and it is now possible to walk behind the fall. The natural auditorium is frequently used in summer for brass band concerts.

Visitors looking for an exhilarating walk can follow the Pennine Way to the summit of Great Shunner Fell and on a clear day this makes an excellent view point. To the south are Whernside, Ingleborough and Pen-y-ghent, but the best views of all are those of the Lakeland fells on the western horizon. The walk up Shunner Fell leaves Hardraw and turns right along the walled lane beyond the Green Dragon.

Wensleydale, like Swaledale, has an old and a new road, but where the Swaledale roads keep swapping sides, the old and the new in Wensleydale keep mostly to their appointed courses; the old in this case being the one on the north side avoiding a river crossing all the way east from Appersett. While traffic hurtles along on the A684 life is more relaxed along the line of the old road. **Askrigg** is typical of the villages north of Ure, a tightly-knit village of 17th and 18th-century houses at the foot of its common land. Two roads from Swaledale join at Askrigg on their descent from Askrigg Common. Askrigg was old before the Normans came and a market was held there until Hawes superseded it. As was the case in other villages around, hand-knitting was a flourishing industry before mechanisation came along. This is 'Herriot' coun-

try; a sturdy cobble-fronted house opposite the ancient church has been used so often as Skeldale House in the *All Creatures Great and Small* TV series, that the name stuck! Two waterfalls nearby are **Mill Gill Force** and **Whitfield Force** and the easy stroll to Mill Gill Force would make a pleasant saunter after lunch in Askrigg. To reach it take the lane behind the church to its end and then cross the beck by a signposted path and on through a pretty wood. Follow the stream as far as the waterfall.

Across the dale and on a tight double bend on the A684 is **Bainbridge**. The present day village is mostly on the west bank of the River Bain, and leaves the relics of Roman Bainbridge for future archaeologists to uncover.*

After the Norman Conquest, Bainbridge was the headquarters of the forest wardens of the Forest of Wensleydale who were charged with protecting it for the king. The forest in this case was the woodland variety but gradual clearances provided farm land for an ever increasing population. The only link with the ancient forest is the custom of blowing a horn at 9pm every night from late September to Shrovetide, to warn travellers still out in the forest.

To the south of Bainbridge, a quiet road through Countersett, a village with long standing Quaker traditions, leads into Raydale and to a natural lake – a rarity in the dales. **Semer Water** was formed during the last Ice Age when a retreating glacier left a moraine, or pile of debris, which acted as a dam. So say the geologists but local lore has a much more romantic legend. This says that there is a drowned village beneath Semer Water. A poor traveller tried to get shelter one wild and stormy

Folklore insists that a drowned village lies beneath Semer Water.

**Mill Gill Force Walk
1 mile – ¹/₂ hour**

*Roman Virosidum, on a high mound above the village of Bainbridge, once held a cohort of 500 men. As the fort is on private land, permission must be sought before entering the site. What little is known of the fort indicates that it was an important outpost guarding Wensleydale. Most of the Roman road can still be traced as the green lane across Cam Fell, then as a metalled road to Ribblehead and beyond.

**Semer Water
1 mile south of Bainbridge.
Access from A684.**

Aysgarth,
Upper Falls.

Aysgarth,
Middle Falls.

Gayle Beck, Hawes.

night, but was refused by all except a shepherd and his wife whose house stood beyond the village. The next morning the traveller laid the following curse:

Semerwater rise - Semerwater sink,
And swallow all the town,
Save yon little house
Where they gave me food and drink

Immediately a tremendous deluge started and drowned all the village and its inhabitants except the kind shepherd and his wife. True or false, the strange twist to this tale is that in 1937 when the level of the lake was lowered in a land reclamation scheme, a Bronze Age village was found beneath the waters. Another story concerns the conspicuous boulder near the lake's outflow. Known as the 'Carlin Stone', it is said to have been thrown there by the Devil, but is part of the moraine dam.

Limestone beds which feature so prominently in the western part of the Dales dip below ground to the east and north-east, but in lower Wensleydale they are visible as the river bed, and what an effect it makes!

Below Aysgarth the river tumbles over three broad steps in the limestone to create the famous **Aysgarth Falls**, one of the most popular picnic spots in the Dales. Paths to the falls are signposted and there is an excellent information centre at the old station and a nature trail through the surrounding woodlands. The obvious power of the river was used to drive the mill, which now houses the Yorkshire Museum of Horse Drawn Carriages. The mill has had a mixed career; a woollen mill, later a flour mill, and it once supplied material for 7,000 red flannel shirts for Italian soldiers of Garibaldi's army. A viewing platform recently added to the museum gives the best views of Aysgarth's Upper Falls, but the Middle and Lower Falls are the most impressive.

Aysgarth village in the *Domesday Book* is recorded as 'Eshescard' meaning 'an open space marked by oaks'. Its church, though built on ancient foundations, is mainly 19th-century and contains medieval woodwork removed from Jervaulx Abbey after the Dissolution. In particular a 15th-century screen, regarded as the finest piece of Cistercian woodwork in North Yorkshire, and a finely carved reading desk are here.

Bishopdale, another of the tributaries of the Ure, is quiet and little known despite having the road from

Aysgarth Falls
$^1/_4$ mile east of Aysgarth. A series of limestone steps create the Upper, Middle and Lower Falls. Information centre, nature trail.
Careful screening of the National Park car park on the site of the old railway station north of the river, ensures that cars do not detract visually from the scenic value of the falls.

The seven-stepped cross in Carperby.

Wharfedale down its length. Few motorists who drive over from Buckden take the trouble to stop and explore its hidden byways, but those who do will be well rewarded. The three Bishopdale villages, **West Burton**, **Thoralby** and **Newbiggin** are clusters of interesting houses, most of them around 220 years old. Both West Burton and Thoralby have pretty waterfalls nearby and a complex of interlinked footpaths weaves in and out of farmsteads on the dale's side. West Burton is built medieval fashion around a wide green, but despite its apparent age does not have a church or a market cross. The stepped obelisk at the head of the village green only dates from 1820. A fieldpath, north from West Burton towards the A684, passes two strange looking towers on private land close to Edgley Farm. Even though they may look like follies, they once served a useful purpose as smoke houses for curing bacon. The track which climbs from Newbiggin above Bishopdale to Wasset Fell was originally used by miners who worked the sparse veins on the fells between Bishopdale and Walden Beck.

In late August **West Witton**, straggling for a mile along the A684, has a traditional bonfire ceremony. The true origin is probably pagan and lost in antiquity, but is known locally as the 'Burning of Owd Bartle' or St Bartholomew, and takes place on the saint's feast day.

West Witton was mentioned in the *Domesday Book* as 'Whittone', a 'stone village'. Penhill to the south of the village is an ancient beacon site, a point for both warning and celebratory fires. A three-quarters of a mile climb from the Melmerby road leads to this vantage point with its views of Wensleydale. A little over a mile west of West Witton and reached by a footpath leaving the A684 at Swinithwaite is the Knights Templar's Chapel, whose scant remains of the Knights Templar, withhold the story of why this enigmatic semi-military order held their devotions in such a remote, but beautiful spot.

Across the shoulder of Penhill is **Coverdale**, the last of the Ure's southern feeders, another of the often ignored places of solitude. The long valley road through its scattered communities offers many rewards to the motorist, but great care must be taken on its descent into Wharfedale down steep Park Rash. This road was once a pack-horse way and the village of Horsehouse in the middle of the dale was a principal resting place before the long haul across the moors to Kettlewell. Pack-horse trains would have crossed the river by the beautiful bridge below the church.

Footpaths which in the old days were made to provide the shortest passage between two places can be used for pleasure today. Two which linked Coverdale to Bishopdale (with careful planning and the use of the OS map), offer an enjoyable day's walk of about 10 miles across Carlton Moor.

Carlton Moor Walk
10 miles – 1 day

Returning to the main dale and travelling north along the road from Aysgarth, the village of **Carperby** proudly boasts the fact that it has twice won the best kept village competition organised by the Yorkshire Rural Community Council. There was once a market here built around the seven-stepped cross which was raised in 1674. Nearby in the fields north of the road can be seen examples of lynchets – horizontal strips ploughed along a hillside in medieval days to provide more arable land.

The first road to be built through Wensleydale kept well above the north bank of the river and wound up and down steep hillsides in a manner which would be unacceptable to motorised traffic. As a result the villages on this side have remained unspoilt with very little development over the years.

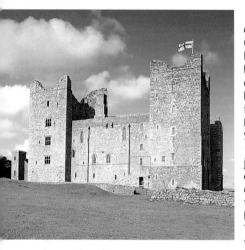

*Castle Bolton** village saw excitement for over a year during the Civil War and it is nice to think that little has happened to it since then. Bolton Castle dominates the western end of this unspoilt village. It was built in 1379 at a cost of £12,000 for the first Lord Scrope, a Chancellor of England. The ill fated Mary, Queen of Scots was lodged here from July 1567 to January 1569 on her slow journey south and eventual execution. Colonel Chaytor held the castle for the Crown against the troops of Oliver Cromwell until forced by starvation to surrender in 1645. The castle remained unoccupied until fairly recently when work was commenced to preserve this fine building.

Above and below: dominating the valley, Bolton Castle.

Castle Bolton is little changed since Mary, Queen of Scots was held captive in its castle.

Castle Bolton
Village and castle 4¹/₂ miles north-east of Aysgarth on Reeth road. Attractive village made up of houses ranging in two rows away from the castle. The great hall and adjacent rooms have been restored. Licensed restaurant.

Across Apedale Beck **Redmire** housed miners who worked the veins of the south side of the Grinton ore field. In 1861 the population was 420 but now it is about half that number. Redmire takes its name from the reedy lake which was to the south of the village until it was drained in the last century. Redmire's church is well worth visiting. Based on a monastic chantry, it escaped destruction during the Reformation to become the parish church. Although it has been altered over the years, much of the Norman fabric remains, the doorway being the best example. Marked on the OS map as 'Old Flue' above Preston-under-Scar, the longest flue in England ran underground from the smelt mill at Keld Heads to Cobscar over half a mile away on the moors to the north. Some of the richest lead veins in Wensleydale were worked around here. Not shown on any OS map are the prehistoric dwellings discovered a little to the east of Preston-under-Scar. The road from Catterick across the scar has the surprise view of Wensleydale from Scarth Nick. Below Redmire, Apedale Beck feeds into the Ure near Redmire Force, the last of the limestone-step waterfalls of Wensleydale.

White Rose Candle Workshop is in Wensley water mill where Mick, Jen and Rachel White have been making candles since 1978.

The dale takes its name from **Wensley**. The village sits astride the A684, an important market until the plague of

1563 wiped out its inhabitants. It is now overshadowed in commercial importance by Hawes, but Wensley is a far prettier place surrounding its ancient village green. The partly restored mill below the bridge near the waterfall and now used as a pottery, was operated by an over-shot waterwheel. The church is one of the most beautiful in the Dales and the most interesting. It escaped the Victorian rebuilding that afflicted many churches in the area and most of what is seen was built in the 13th and 15th centuries, the date of much of its fine woodwork.*

Bolton Hall, home of Lord Bolton has its main gates in the centre of Wensley and there are public footpaths through the beautiful parkland of the hall, though the hall itself is not open. The hall was built in 1678 to replace Bolton Castle after it became untenable following the Civil War. It was first owned by Charles Powlett who later became the Duke of Bolton, and was partially rebuilt earlier this century after a serious fire.

The substantial village of **Leyburn**, recorded in the Domesday Book as 'le Borne' or 'the stream by the clearing' sits well above and to the north of the Ure. It had its market charter granted by Charles II and in 1686 market day was changed from Tuesday to Friday. Five busy roads meeting at Leyburn have contributed to its development. From the west end of the market place a footpath leads to the wooded crag of Leyburn Shawl. Remains of ancient earthworks surround the crag and prehistoric implements have been found nearby. A spot known as 'Queen's Gap' on the Shawl is supposed to be where Mary, Queen of Scots was recaptured after only 2 hours freedom during her imprisonment in Bolton Castle.

Roger Hansell, one of England's most prominent violin makers, has his studio workshop by the eastern outskirts of Leyburn. Here you can see the traditional methods of violin making, unchanged since the days of Stradivari. Swineside ceramics are also nearby, making and displaying teapots of every conceivable shape and size.

Middleham is linked to Leyburn by an iron girder bridge built by public subscription in 1850, replacing an earlier suspension bridge which collapsed in 1831 after only two years' use. The impressive ruins of **Middleham Castle** date from 1170, and three centuries later it became home for the future Richard III.* The keep is original and despite being made untenable after Richard's defeat on Bosworth Field in 1485, the castle

*The church's beautifully carved screen, which came from Easby Abbey (near Richmond), stands behind the Bolton Box Pew, while near the church door is a reliquary, also from Easby Abbey and said to be the only one of its kind in England. It may have held the remains of St Agatha, their patron saint. The finely carved choir stalls were made in 1527 by the same carvers who worked on Ripon Cathedral. Peter Goldsmith, who was the surgeon on board HMS Victory and in whose arms Lord Nelson died at Trafalgar came from Wensley and is buried in the churchyard.

Leyburn Teapottery
Witty and unique designs hand-made on the premises.
Middleham Castle
On A6018, 2 miles south-east of Leyburn. One of the largest keeps in England.

*King Richard III became the owner of Middleham Castle in 1471, through his marriage to Anne, daughter of Richard Neville, Earl of Warwick, the 'Kingmaker'. It is a pleasant thought to see King Richard resting at Middleham between phases of the power struggle that became known as the 'Wars of the Roses'. His son Edward was born at Middleham, but died aged 12; his room can still be seen in the castle ruins.

Above left, Middleham Castle, above right, the keep.

ruins are in a fine state of preservation, a true memorial to the medieval stone-masons who built it. King Richard's crest was a white boar, one of which, very much worn with age, still decorates the Swine Cross in the market place. Another feature of the town is St Alkelda's Well, named after the martyred Saxon princess who died at the hands of the Danes rather than renounce her Christian beliefs. Middleham is also a racehorse training town with a dozen trainers handling several hundred horses, often to be seen at exercise on Middleham Moor to the west.

Across Coverdale, tree-lined **East Witton** is built on a crossroads of two minor roads, with the A6108, formerly the coach road from York to Kendal, taking a right-angled bend through the village. Sleepy now, it has had a market charter since 1306 and the Poll Tax of 1379 shows 220 tax paying inhabitants.

A minor road leaves the A6108 about half a mile north of East Witton, to cross the Ure into **Spennithorne**. This village has changed little in size since Ralph Fitz Randolph built a castle there in 1194. Only a few stones remain, but from them it is possible to conjure the impression of a fair-sized fortress. The village churchyard boasts a Russian cross from Sebastopol, erected by a member of the local Van Straubenzee family, who fought at Sebastopol in the Crimean War.

Below **Middleham** the valley widens and its character becomes more wooded. The ruins of Jervaulx Abbey are about three miles from Middleham along the Masham road. It was built in the 12th century by Cistercian monks originally from Fors in France, who moved there from the then inhospitable area around Askrigg. The monks made a special cheese, a forerunner to Wensleydale, from ewes' milk. The scant ruins of Jervaulx Abbey remain in mute testimony to Henry VIII's determination to crush the power of the monasteries. In 1536 the Pilgrimage of Grace started from here, led unwillingly by the abbot, Adam Sedburgh. The pilgrims hoped to persuade the king away from his policy of destroying the monasteries, but he tricked them by offering a pardon. As soon as they made to return to their dales he took revenge. Adam Sedburgh was imprisoned in the Tower of London, where his name can still be seen scratched on a wall. He was executed at Tyburn in 1537 and Jervaulx was destroyed. All that is left of this once extensive religious house are a few graceful arches and stone pillars still peacefully mouldering into tranquil antiquity.

Ex-servicemen and women can spend a nostalgic hour or so at the privately run Museum of Badges and Battledress at Crakehall on the A684, four miles north-west of **Bedale**. Fortunately for Bedale the A1, the Great

Jervaulx Abbey was founded by Cistercian monks in the 12th century.

Jervaulx Abbey
5 miles south-east of Leyburn. Several ancient gravestones and the remains of the 15th-century kitchen can be seen.

126

Bedale Hall Museum
Junction of A684 and
B6268. Hall dates from
17th century. Georgian
ballroom with fine
Italian plaster ceiling and
rare floor. Museum
displays local arts and
crafts, tradesmen's tools,
clocks, coins,
weights etc.

*(1) Fitz Randolph of
Middleham Castle built
another of his fortresses
in Snape and through
various marriages it
became the property of
Catherine Parr, the last
of the wives of
Henry VIII, whom she
survived.*

*(2) A survey of 1811
shows Snape having
four inns, a poorhouse
and a lock-up known as
the Black Hole!*

North Road, is well to the east and as a result traffic noise has no effect on this quiet market town. Featured in the Domesday Book, it has held a Tuesday market around its slender stepped cross since 1251. Sited on gently rising land between the lower reaches of Swaledale and Wensleydale, the town was once an important commercial centre, connecting the central dales with east coast ports. An imaginative scheme, which came to nothing, planned to canalise Bedale Beck and so connect the town to the navigable Swale. All that is left are incongruous mooring rings and the grandiose title of The Harbour given to an area around Bedale Mill. Water still powers this mill, the last in Bedale.

St Gregory's, Bedale's parish church, has a mixture of styles but the largest of its bells hung in Jervaulx Abbey over 400 years ago. The bell tower was used as a lookout against raiding Scots in the 14th century. Nearby Bedale Hall is Georgian, a fine setting for the local government officials to work in. Three miles south of Bedale, the tiny village of **Snape** has an almost park-like aspect. An avenue of trees planted in 1701 lead into this village whose roots go back to the 12th century. *(1) Snape's prosperity was based on woolcombing, but with the centralising of the Yorkshire wool trade on industrial towns of the West Riding, the village declined.*(2) Thorpe Perrow, home of the Danbys, is close by and its famous Arboretum is open from mid-March to the end of October.

The Bedale Hunt uses the broad acres between the A1 and Wensleydale. Parkland and ancestral homes dot this prosperous landscape; many of the houses open their gardens throughout the summer, but it is best to check the details locally.

A minor road south of Thorpe Perrow to the B6267, makes a curious dog-leg through a pretty village called **Well**. The unusual name refers to St Michael's Well, which has been a site of veneration since pagan times, part of a complex of henges and tumuli in the surrounding area. A prosperous Roman built a luxurious villa near the well and decorated it with the tessellated pavement now on display in the parish church. At the time of the Domesday survey the church was only a wooden structure and the present building has Norman foundations. Little remains from that era apart from the dog-tooth working around the doorway, following

Scottish raids around 1318. The font cover dates from 1352, one of the oldest in England and was the gift of Ralph Neville, Lord of Middleham who was responsible for rebuilding the church. A row of alms houses near the church which were built in 1758 are linked with a charity originally endowed by Ralph Neville.

Devotees of 'real ale' make the pilgrimage to **Masham**, for this is the home of one of the oldest and truest brews, Theakston's 'Old Peculier'; the spelling is correct, a 'peculier' was a kind of medieval weights and measures official. Masham guards a crossing of the Ure on its southerly course into the Vale of York. Its church contains some Norman work but has been Victorianised; its best features are the octagonal 15th-century lantern and tall spire topping a Norman tower and the inside has many unspoilt features dating as far back as the 11th century. A venerable stone column decorated with the twelve apostles and the Adoration of the Magi standing in the churchyard, is probably 7th-century. A market has been held at Masham since 1250, and the huge market place gives an air of spaciousness to the town. The imposing market cross once incorporated a bull ring and a set of stocks. Masham's big annual event is a traction engine rally and steam fair which is held on a nearby meadow. Uredale Glass is near the King's Head in Masham where beautifully coloured hand-crafted glass is made. The Black Sheep Brewery is also at Masham and its Visitor Centre is open for most of the year.

Masham
Black Sheep Brewery, Wellgarth, Masham. Traditional brewing, tastings, bistro and shop.

Masham workshops
Glass making, hand-made jewellery and pottery.

Colsterdale joins Wensleydale just below Masham, one of the least known and yet arguably one of the prettiest of Wensleydale's tributary dales. Its river, the Burn, starts its life to the west, high on Great Haw and near to where the monks of Jervaulx Abbey mined coal and ironstone, smelting the metal lower down the dale. Swinton Castle, known locally as the 'Tea Caddy Castle' and now used as a college, stands within attractive parkland above the south bank of the Burn.

Grewelthorpe and Kirkby Malzeard are two villages in the middle of a 'cat's cradle' of by ways south of the main dale. The former, **Grewelthorpe** has a pretty village pond which is probably a flooded gravel pit; 'grewel' is an old word for gravel.*

Kirkby Malzeard was recorded in the *Domesday Book* as the 'church in the forest clearing'. The forest is long gone, but the village retains its quiet charm despite

*Four hundred years ago, the women of Grewelthorpe, losing patience at their menfolk's delay over disputed coal mining rights, fought a bloody battle with their neighbours from Kirkby Malzeard. The resulting settlement still allows both lots of villagers to gather coal beneath Grewelthorpe Moor but few, if any, still bother.

Narrow back streets lead to Ripon's Minster.

20th-century pressures. The parish church was once known as the 'Queen of the Moors' but most of the present structure is the result of rebuilding following a disastrous fire in 1908. Mowbray Castle was to the east of the church but, as the stone cross in the churchyard explains, it was destroyed by order of Henry II in 1173. Edward I granted a charter to hold a weekly market but it is a long time since one was held. The market cross is a replica, the original being destroyed by a local worthy in 1866. He considered it an eyesore, a sentiment not accepted by the rest of the village who promptly set about building the present cross!

Moving downstream again, the A6108 crosses the river by an ancient bridge to enter **West Tanfield**, a village to delight the eye. Marmion Tower dominates the scene, the gatehouse of a vanished ancestral home. Sir Walter Scott based his novel *Marmion* on the family, but there is no record of any Marmion being at the Battle of Flodden.

Ripon can claim to be one of England's oldest boroughs with a history closely linked to its church for thirteen centuries. "In 650, St Wilfrid became bishop and built its first church soon afterwards. Alfred the Great granted the town its charter in 886." The crypt still survives and can be visited beneath the present central tower. Today's Minster, raised to cathedral status in 1836, contains some fine ecclesiastical woodwork together with one of the greatest of our early English west fronts.

Ripon
Cathedral dates from 672. Rich ecclesiastical treasure displayed in the Saxon crypt.

Norton Conyers
3½ miles north of Ripon, off A61. Fine Jacobean manor house belonging to the Grahams, who still live there, since 1624. Exhibition of pictures, furniture and wedding dresses. Walled garden.

As a religious centre in its own right, as well as being close to Fountains Abbey's monastic influence, conveniently placed between the pastoral countryside of Wensleydale, Nidderdale and the rich arable lands of the Vale of York, Ripon soon acquired charters for markets and fairs. It developed round the twin centres of Minster and market place, the two parts of the town most attractive to visitors. The medieval street pattern is still based on these areas, but most of Ripon's attractive buildings are the result of Georgian and Victorian growth. In the centre of the market place is an impressive obelisk of 1781, and on the south side the elegant town hall of 1801 almost overshadows a surviving half-timbered building, the 16th-century Wakeman's House, formerly the home of Hugh Ripley, who died in 1637 – the last wakeman and Ripon's first mayor. One of the wakeman's duties was that of horn blower, a custom still continued each evening at 9pm, when he blows a horn at each corner of the market place, and outside the house of the current mayor wherever he or she resides. The Ure is navigable as far as Ripon, the town being connected to the main river by canal, and a busy marina makes an attractive foreground to the town. There is a racetrack on water-meadows between the canal and the river where meetings are held throughout the year. Ripon Law and Order Museum in St Marygate together with the Workhouse Museum on Allhallowsgate, are a link with earlier attitudes towards the punishment of criminals and vagrancy.

Fountains Abbey, founded in 1132 on what was then a wild site by the little River Skell, became one of the richest of all Cistercian monasteries. Today, in the setting of an 18h-century landscaped park, its ruins are probably the most beautiful and certainly the most extensive, of any Cistercian foundation in Britain. Tranquil and serene it may be today, but Fountains had its share of troubles. The thirteen monks from the Benedictine abbey of St Mary's in York found their chosen site (a thorn filled barren wilderness), and at first lived under an elm tree, and amongst the surrounding rocks. After 15 year's work, in 1147 someone maliciously set fire to the abbey and with the exception of the church everything had to be rebuilt. By 1478 records show that the church was in a bad state of repair and work began on the great tower. The worst time for Fountains' history was during the reign of Henry VIII. In

Lightwater Valley Country Theme Park
3 miles north of Ripon on A6108. Adventure park, knuckle-straining rides, farm, shops etc.

Wakeman's House Museum
Market square, Ripon. Building dating from the 14th century. Residence of the 'wakeman' or nightwatchman in medieval times. Now houses an information centre and museum of local crafts and history.

Fountains Abbey and Studley Royal
3 miles south-west of Ripon, off the B6265 to Pateley Bridge.
The largest monastic ruin in Britain.

Fountains Abbey.

1536, Abbot William Thirsk was executed for taking part in the Pilgrimage of Grace and his successor, Marmaduke Bradley, no doubt a King's man, meekly surrendered the abbey to its ultimate fate on 26 November 1539.

The riverside below Fountains Abbey opens out into ornamental gardens and ponds full of exotic geese and visiting water birds. This is **Studley Royal** park created in the 1720s by John Aislabie as a deer park near his house, of which only the stable block remains. The park is part of an estate sold to Sir Richard Gresham in 1540 following the dissolution of Fountains Abbey. Studley Royal is now administered as a country park by North Yorkshire County Council. A short stroll which takes in the glories of the abbey and the beauty of Studley starts at the abbey car park and follows the Skell past Fountains Hall to the abbey. It continues down stream past Half Moon Pound and through the ornamental gardens of the park to follow the canal to the lake with its numerous geese and ducks, both wild and tame. Take plenty of time over this stroll, maybe combining it with a riverside picnic. In the late summer and early autumn the abbey ruins are floodlit. There is partial access by wheelchair to most of the paths surrounding the abbey.

**Fountains Abbey and Studley Royal Walk
2 miles – 1 ¹/₂ hours**

Reached by a turning off the A61 Harrogate road, **Markenfield Hall** is over 400 years old, the finest example of a moated farmhouse in the North. The last Markenfield had to flee the country in 1569 after taking part in the abortive 'Rising of the North'. Fortunately kept in good repair by subsequent owners it remains 'the most complete example of a country gentleman's home since Plantagenet days'.

Newby Hall, the exquisite Queen Anne mansion enriched by the designer Robert Adam, is open to the public and the house contains a priceless collection of works of art, tapestries and artistic furnishings set out in opulent, yet homely surroundings.

The final place in Wensleydale before the Ure joins the Swale is **Boroughbridge**, once a busy staging post on the Great North Road and even now scarcely by-passed by roaring traffic on the A1.

Markenfield Hall
about 2 miles south of Ripon.

Newby Hall
4 miles south-east of Ripon, off Borough-bridge old road. Built in 1690s for Sir Edward Blackett, then redesigned in the 18th century by Robert Adam. Works of art, sculptures and valuable furnishings fill the hall. House and landscaped gardens open to the public. Children's adventure playground. Miniature steam railway.

Three huge stones standing beside the A1 are the sole survivors of seven. Known locally as the 'Devil's Arrows', they show that man has lived here since prehistoric times. Roman conquerers built *Isurium* here on Dere Street, the forerunner of the A1. The site of the fort including an amphitheatre, covers an area of about 60 acres and from the number of artefacts found on site it obviously had great strategic importance. Many of these, together with several finely decorated pavements, can be seen in the small museum on the site.

Whitfield Gill near Askrigg.

Nidderdale & Wharfedale

A short step across the moor from Skell Dale and Fountains Abbey, the character changes yet again in this, the shortest of the main dales. Nidderdale packs a great deal of interest into its length and also provides drinking water for the densely populated regions to its south. Strangely, even though its beauty compares favourably with the main dales, Nidderdale is excluded from the Yorkshire Dales National Park. As a result it is often ignored by visitors and so can be less crowded during the more popular holiday periods.

Glacial action in the Ice Age carved a deep gorge through the easily worn limestone, widening and deepening a course for the River Wharfe. Left to its own devices, the river meanders gently along the dale bottom for most of the year. This gentleness is something of a sham, for in spate after rapidly melting snow or a cloudburst, the Wharfe can become a dangerous river.

Kilnsey Crag.

How Stean Gorge.

Nidderdale

Approach the dale by the back road from Masham in Wensleydale, past **Leighton Reservoir,** then over Ouster Bank and steeply down to Lofthouse. The road continues as a narrow toll road to Scar House and Angram reservoirs almost at the dale head. Cars must be left at the first reservoir as Angram may only be visited on foot.

Middlesmoor is reached by a steep winding road from Lofthouse. This high airy settlement has existed at least since Saxon times, as shown by the ancient font in the village church. Across the valley is the spectacular **How Stean Gorge** which has been developed as a visitor centre. Footbridges on different levels allow access across the deep chasm and there is a children's play area nearby. Tom Taylor's Chamber, a nearby cave, is named after a local rogue who once took refuge in it, and is where in the last century a hoard of Roman coins was found.

The moors on either side of Nidderdale are mostly privately owned and as a result have very restricted public access. There is, however, an excellent ancient high level way which climbs out of the dale above the top reservoirs and crosses the northern flank of Great Whernside before descending to Starbotton in Wharfedale.

How Stean Gorge
10 miles north-west of Pateley Bridge on the Upper Nidderdale road. Narrow gorge with public access by a series of footbridges. Children's play area, car park. Open all the year.

Nidderdale and Wharfedale

**Brimham Rocks,
Pateley Bridge.**

Down the valley, **Ramsgill** at the northern end of Gouthwaite Reservoir, has a church, once an outlying chapel of Byland Abbey where the heathen dale dwellers of early times were converted to Christianity.

After the Ice Age, debris left by the retreating glaciers in Nidderdale blocked the flow of the river and for a time there was a natural lake until erosion released its waters. When Bradford Corporation decided to build **Gouthwaite Reservoir** the story was brought full circle with the second flooding of what should rightly be Gouthwaite Lake. Not only does the water add to the attractive scenery of the dale, but wild birds and waterfowl have colonised the shores and the area has been designated a nature reserve run by the Yorkshire Naturalists' Trust.

**Gouthwaite Reservoir
Nature Reserve**
4 miles north-west of
Pateley Bridge on the
Nidderdale road.
Reservoir, bird sanctuary
and wildfowl, etc. View
from road side.

Quiet **Wath** enjoys a secluded position below Gouthwaite Reservoir, its hotel a perfect base from which to explore Upper Nidderdale. **Foster Beck Mill** on the opposite side of the valley is now an inn, but still retains its huge cast-iron waterwheel in full working order.

Pateley Bridge occupies a sheltered situation facing south-west, making it an ideal suntrap, so it is small wonder that it has become such a popular spot for caravanners and picnickers. It is also a convenient centre for the south-east dales. The small town is old, it was granted a market charter in the 14th century and although the street market was abandoned some time ago, there are still fortnightly sheep sales and an annual agricultural show. There is a signpost marked 'Panorama Walk' in Pateley Bridge; follow it uphill above the town to link up with an easy and level path which commands the extensive view of Nidderdale and the moors beyond.

Lead ore was mined in the dale, mostly around **Greenhow Hill**, south of the B6265 road where the 9-mile long Bycliffe vein was worked. Smelting was carried out on the opposite side of the dale below Brimham Rocks at a place now recognised only by the name of Smelthouses. The local ore had a comparatively high silver content and was much prized by the Romans who mined in this area. A pig (ingot) of Greenhow lead from the first century AD is now at Ripley Castle and another in the British Museum.

The busy but pleasant B6265 was built as a turnpike road between Knaresborough and Grassington to help move fuel and stores in and lead out of the area. In 1858 a party of lead miners discovered a natural cavern which has since been developed as a show cave known as the **Stump Cross Caverns**. The system is over three miles long, but only the show cave is open to the public. This is floodlit to highlight the marvellous stalagmites and stalactites and other rock formations.

Back across the dale below Pateley Bridge and a little to the south-east of the B6265 are the rock formations of **Brimham Rocks**. These are a series of peculiarly shaped Millstone Grit outcrops sculptured into fantastic shapes by the erosion of softer layers topped by harder rocks. Most have names, some are fanciful but others are more easily identifiable such as the 'Dancing Bear' and the precariously perched 'Idol Rock' which, although weighing several tons, is perched on a pedestal about a foot in diameter. The best way to see Brimham Rocks is on foot after parking in one of the well placed car parks off the road between the B6265 and Summer Bridge. The National Trust who own the area, have erected large scale maps showing the positions and names of the various rocks. The best way is to follow their suggested itinerary and walk round the strange formations in a clockwise direction. There is an information centre at Brimham House and a refreshment hut nearby.

Pateley Bridge 'Panorama Walk' 2 miles – 1 hour

Dancing Bear, Brimham Rocks.

Stump Cross Caverns
5 miles west of Pateley Bridge on B6265. Show caves open to the public, access from road, car parking. Visitor centre, café, gift shop.

Brimham Rocks
2 miles south-east of Pateley Bridge. Natural rock sculptures. All information available at Brimham House in the centre of the rocks. Refreshments. Car parking on perimeter, access to spectacular rock formations on foot only. Limited wheel-chair access.

Stocks and village cross, Ripley.

Penitent's cross, Ripley.

Ripley
On A61, 3¹/₂ miles north of Harrogate. Attractive squire's village with architectural curiosities. 14th-century Ripley Castle open to the public.

The B6165 makes a wide sweep above the dale, keeping roughly parallel with the river. At its highest point the name **Burnt Yates** is intriguing; probably a contraction of 'Boundary Gates', for the village once marked the boundary of the lands of Fountains Abbey and the Forest of Knaresborough. The tiny village school was founded in 1750. Endowments of the time allowed for thirty poor boys to be taught the Three R's and thirty poor girls to be instructed in needlework and spinning.

Ripley, across the moors and at the junction of the B6165 with the A61, is an ancient village and was mentioned in the *Domesday Book*. Fortunately it is now spared the heavy traffic of the A61 since a by-pass was built. Oliver Cromwell stayed here after the battle of Marston Moor. The village has a French look about it, and no wonder, for it was modelled on one in Alsace-Lorraine for Sir William Amcotts Ingilby in 1827. The French similarity is complete right down to the *hôtel de ville*, or town hall, which was added in 1854. The money to rebuild the village was raised from the sale of an outlying farm, now the town centre of Harrogate! No longer in any danger from through traffic, visitors can wander round Ripley's cobbled market square with its cross and venerable stocks.

The Ingilby family have been associated with Ripley since the 14th century. Their home, Ripley Castle, is open to the public and is at the lower end of the village beyond the

14th-century church with its 'Weeping Cross'. Apparently the name comes from the action of penitents who confessed their sins at its base.

Valley Gardens, Harrogate.

Two more Nidderdale villages are worthy of a mention. **Birstwith**, now popular with Harrogate commuters, is where Charlotte Brontë spent an unhappy holiday at Swarcliffe Hall when she was a governess. **Hampsthwaite** has a charter granted by Edward I and was an important river crossing from Roman times – a pack-horse bridge still spans the river.

The spa town of **Harrogate** flourished until the beginning of the 20th century and then fell into a decline after World War I. By adopting its present role as a dormitory to the commercial cities of Yorkshire, as well as developing its own identity and modern character, the town still retains an unrivalled popularity as a health and pleasure resort. Over the years Harrogate has developed important conference facilities and also attracted many high class shops to its elegant Victorian high street. Remnants of the spa can still be seen in places such as the Opera House and Royal Baths. The Royal Pump Room with its Sulphur Well has been preserved as a museum of life in a spa as it would have been during the Victorian hey-day of the town. A legacy of the more gentle days of Harrogate lies in the number of parks and open spaces such as the Stray, a 200-acre open space

Harrogate
Museum, art gallery, Harlow Car Gardens, Stray, Rudding Park.

**Above and below:
House in the Rock,
Knaresborough.**

**Knaresborough
Old Court House
Museum**, 14th-century
building, now housing a
reconstructed court room
scene of 1602.

**Fort Montague or
House in the Rock**
18th-century house
carved from solid rock
overlooking the
River Nidd.

almost surrounding the town centre and jealously preserved by the inhabitants. On the western edge of Harrogate are the famous Harlow Car Gardens, owned by the Northern Horticultural Society. A never ending display of colour flourishes throughout the year, ranging from spring flowers to rhododendrons, alpines and then roses, for which Harlow Car is particularly famous; all vying in colourful competition with displays of exotic flowers and herbaceous borders. Harlow Car also has a more serious purpose, being used as a trial ground for new fruit and vegetable plants suited to northern weather conditions.

To the north-east and almost totally on the north bank of the River Nidd, is the old town of **Knaresborough**. The Romans are thought to have built a fort here, but it grew mainly in Anglo-Saxon times with the development of a castle to protect against Viking raids. The ruins that are seen today are of a 12th-century castle left more or less as it was after Cromwell made it useless during the Civil War. Knaresborough has many interesting buildings and features, such as the oldest chemist's shop in England, along with the Old Court House Museum and a house **Fort Montague**, carved out of the solid rock overlooking the Nidd. Visit **Mother Shipton's Cave** where Mother Shipton, in the 15th century, prophesied the coming of aeroplanes, iron ships, motor cars, men walking under water and many other inventions and events such as world wars. She was born in this cave near the Dropping Well on the banks of the Nidd. In the Dropping Well inanimate articles are coated with limestone from lime-laden water dropping from the roof of the crag and appear to be turned to stone. Rowing boats can be hired to enjoy the tranquil stretch of the Nidd beneath the shadow of **Knaresborough Castle**, or for the less energetic, a simple stroll by the river completes the pleasures of Nidderdale.

Turning west and back to the more central dales, the A59 Harrogate to Skipton road crosses short Washburn Dale, now mostly flooded to provide drinking water for Leeds and Bradford and with quaintly named Blubberhouses as its only village. Minor roads criss-cross the dale and the B6451, Dangerous Corner to Otley road, crosses the neck of Lindley Wood Reservoir, but to really explore this almost lost valley, it will be necessary to follow the many rights-of-way on foot. One possibility is to use public footpaths radiating from the remote village of Timble to reach Swinsty Reservoir and maybe continue further down the dale to Lindley Wood. **Timble** is about a mile east of the minor road from Blubberhouses to Otley. The village has one pub and parking should be easy to find.

Wharfedale

T he long distance Dales Way Walk follows Wharfedale for a good third of its length. The route starts at Ilkley and follows the dale all the way through Grassington, Kettlewell and Buckden before meeting the Pennine Way for a short distance above Ribblehead. After a sharp dog-leg on Cam Fell the path continues through Dent and Sedbergh into the Lune Valley and across the M6 by the Crook of Lune. The last lap is through the Lakeland foothills around the River Kent and finally to Bowness on Windermere. As a walk it does not have half the rigours of the Pennine Way and its length of 73 miles is often scoffed at by long distance walkers, but for scenery there can be no finer walk especially if taken in short easy stages. It can be easily split over many separate days or taken over a short holiday week. Time on a walk like this should be of

The long distance Dales Way Walk 73 miles

Tin Bridge, Linton Falls.

Limestone pavement near Yockenthwaite.

no consequence. Apart from the 15 miles from Sedbergh to Burnside accommodation and refreshment stops are relatively easy to find and should not cause problems for anyone who prefers to walk without too many prior arrangements and bookings.

The River Wharfe starts its life in Langstrothdale high on the moors of Cam Pasture and shares its birthplace with the Ribble. Quickly flowing south, the river flows past settlements which, within the memory of men not long dead, were still used as summer farms in the Scandinavian method of farming. The first hamlet in the ancient Forest of Langstroth is **Oughtershaw** where its hall was built centuries ago. Next at the foot of forested Greenfield Beck is **Beckermonds** (or Beggarmuns as the locals call it). The river flows through Yockenthwaite, a Norse-Irish name for the 'clearing of Eogan', and near to where Bronze Age people built a mysterious cairned circle. Ever widening, it runs on past Deepdale to **Hubberholme**, named after 'Hubba' the Viking chief who once controlled this part of Wharfedale. Hubberholme is one of those tiny places often ignored, but with its own inimitable appeal. The pride and joy of the village is the beautiful Norman church of St Michael, once a chapel of ease to the main church at Arncliffe. Inside is a rare medieval rood loft painted in red, black and gold. Other woodwork is mostly modern and is the work of Robert Thompson of Kilburn whose trade mark is the carved mouse which you will find hidden in out-of-the-way corners.*

The river makes a sharp turn southwards between Hubberholme and Buckden and the widening valley bottom gives a sheltered site for the first of Wharfedale's picture postcard villages, **Buckden**. Like most of the dale's villages, Buckden was settled by the Norsemen, but they only developed a more sophisticated husbandry on the land already partly settled by earlier man. In the 12th century, Buckden became the residence of officials controlling the Forest of Langstroth. In later years the village developed as a social centre of the upper dale, a tradition which continues to this day. At one time the inn doubled as a wool sale room and is where some of the old weighing equipment survives.

That intrepid 17th-century traveller, Lady Anne Clifford, came this way on a journey of inspection of her northern estates. She climbed from Buckden across Buckden Raikes going steeply above the village and then across Stake Moss to Bainbridge. She, not unnaturally, felt that this was one of the most dangerous places she had ever visited. The road she followed is now superseded by the B6160, but the original builders of this track were Roman. On an airy ledge below the point where the old and new roads join, the upland community of **Cray** clusters around the welcoming sight of the White Lion Inn. The climb from Buckden to Cray is still steep, but the modern road, especially in summer, holds none of the terrors Lady Anne Clifford experienced.

Starbotton was developed by the Saxons, but grew with the discovery of lead on Cam Head Moor near a curious boundary ditch built in prehistoric times. The village is recorded in the *Domesday Book*, but in 1686 the worst recorded flood in Wharfedale's history wiped out practically the whole village. Only a handful of houses prior to that date remain.

There is a short but steep climb to the eastern fells above Starbotton. The view down Wharfedale will make the effort seem little. The path follows a route straight up the side of Cam Gill Beck across the curiously named Knuckle Bone Pasture to Starbotton Fell. Here the track divides, and one must follow the right hand path over Starbotton Out Moor to join the walled access lane from Cam Head Beck back to Starbotton.

*The George Inn across the valley was once owned by the church and every New Year's Day the vicar would officiate over a kind of parliament when the 'poor pasture' was let for the benefit of the local poor. This 1,000 year-old custom still operates, but is now in the hands of a local auctioneer.

Eastern fell Walk
3¹/₂ miles – 2 hours

Park Rash road climbs steeply out of Kettlewell.

The road from Wharfedale to Coverdale which starts in Kettlewell was once used to test the climbing ability of cars up the notorious **Park Rash**, parts of which have a gradient of 1 in 4. For a short while it was on the coach route between London and Richmond via Skipton, but was found to be so difficult that it was abandoned. The valley road skirts Kettlewell and crosses the Wharfe by a lovely old bridge where the masons who built it left a wealth of their coded marks.

Kettlewell is Norse for 'bubbling spring' and makes a handy base for a weekend's exploration along a whole series of footpaths and tracks radiating from either side of the village. Some were old routes to other villages, giving access to high pasture, or were lead miners' tracks. Others which appear to end abruptly, were sledge roads used to bring peat down from the high tops in the days when this valuable and accessible fuel was used extensively throughout the Dales.

Narrow terraced fields around Kettlewell and other Dales' villages are known as 'lynchets' and were created as ploughable strips as far back as the Middle Ages. The parish church is built on Norman foundations, although the present structure is early Victorian. Stand at the roadside, a little way beyond the 'Kettlewell' sign at the Starbotton end of the village, and wait for a lull in the traffic. On a calm day there is a remarkable echo from this point.

The long moorland ridge of Old Cote Moor, west of Kettlewell, divides Wharfedale from its tributary

Littondale. Its river, the Skirfare, drains the northern slopes of **Fountains Fell** and Pen-y-ghent. Although very similar in character to the main dale, Littondale is almost a hidden gem with the main village of Arncliffe and its satellites Hawkswick, Litton, and Halton Gill spaced at regular intervals on either side of it along the dale bottom. The valley road continues with a struggle over the steep sides of Pen-y-ghent to Stainforth in Ribblesdale and a branch road from Arncliffe provides an even greater challenge of steep switchbacks below Fountains Fell before timid motorists can thankfully arrive in Malham and safety. Pack-horse trains once used the green lane from Halton Gill to Horton-in-Ribblesdale, but now it makes a quiet path across the northern shoulder of Pen-y-ghent. Halton Gill would have been a much busier place during the hey-day of pack-horse trains; the road from Stainforth was originally one of their trails and another, now a footpath, climbed from Yockenthwaite in nearby Wharfedale by way of the 1,000ft high pass across Horse Head Moor.

Halton Gill is not the most isolated dwelling place in the Dales; the lonely farmstead of Cash House, two miles above Foxup at the confluence of the two streams which make the Skirfare, has the rare privilege of being the remotest house in this part of Yorkshire. The 17th-century chapel of Halton Gill is combined with the schoolhouse.

The concave eastern slopes of Darnbrook Fell, Fountains Fell's eastern outlier, dominate **Litton**. This pleasantly sited village which gives its name to the dale was part of the lands of Fountains Abbey. Litton marked the western boundary of their wealth-generating sheep walk.*

Arncliffe, the name is old Norse and is said to relate to eagles nesting on the local scars, is mostly built around an attractive village green. The church was first built in the 12th century, although the present building has stood since 1796. The names of Littondale men who fought the Scots at Flodden Field in 1513 are recorded inside the church; names on the list which will still bring a response from their descendants who live in the dale.

Walkers can enjoy the beauty of Littondale and its river by following the path from Litton as far as Arncliffe and then on to Hawkswick on the north bank. Paths link Halton Gill with Hubberholme, Litton with Buckden and Arncliffe with Starbotton; all the second named villages being in Wharfedale. A combination of any two paths can be used to make a really good round trip walk.

*Coal was mined on the summit of Fountains Fell from shallow bell shaped pits. They can still be traced as shallow depressions and nearby is the sturdy stone structure which was used as a coke oven.

Littondale Walk
4 miles – 2 hours

Kilnsey Fishery.

Hawkswick, the lowest village of Littondale, can claim to have been occupied by man since at least the Iron Age. A number of their sites have been found around the village and Dowkabottom, high to the south-west, was inhabited until the 4th century. Hawkswick Cote along with Arncliffe Cote, were former grange farms belonging to Fountains Abbey. Wild Littondale joins Wharfedale, the waters of Skirfare mingling with the main river at Amerdale Dub, a favourite hiding place for trout.

Motorists travelling down Wharfedale from its junction with Littondale soon see the remarkable 170ft high **Kilnsey Crag**. Overhanging 40ft, its receding lower part was carved by glacial action during the last Ice Age. The crag overshadows the annual Kilnsey Show at the end of August. Kilnsey is at the eastern end of Mastiles Lane, a green road over the limestone moors to Malham, fortunately still resisting proposals to upgrade it to a motor road. Once owned by Fountains Abbey which had a grange here, it has seen busier times; once there were corn and textile mills. Now, limestone is quarried behind the crag and a trout farm has been established down the road from the crag. Known as Kilnsey Water Park, not only is it operated as a commercial trout farm, but there is also an extensive aquarium, water garden centre, angling areas and landscaped ponds where visitors can feed the energetic trout and other fishes.

Across the dale from Kilnsey, is **Conistone**, a village which can trace its history back to Saxon times. Conistone's church is probably the oldest in Wharfedale, certainly the least 'improved' by our Victorian forebears. Behind the village is the narrow and impressive limestone gorge of **Gurling Trough**.

The large area of woodland south of Conistone is all that remains of the forest which once filled Wharfedale. **Grass Wood** together with the adjacent Bastow Wood is a nature reserve. Fascinating plant life abounds in the reserve, an unspoilt relic of our ancient woodland. Just inside the south-east corner of Grass Wood, a series of mounds are all that is left of a medieval village obliterated by the Black Death. Even though a public right-of-way passes through Grass Wood and visitors are welcomed, it is on the strict understanding that no flowers are taken or trees damaged. Dogs must be on a lead and on no account should any fires be started.

Man's exploitation of the fells above Grassington has its greatest impact west of the B6265. A huge limestone quarry based on Cracoe defaces the landscape in answer to the insatiable demands for better roads. The men of Cracoe who died in both world wars are remembered by a stone column high on a fell to the south. On the scarred fells to the north-east all is now silent, but lead was mined in quantity under **Grassington Moor** until the late 19th century. Levels were driven for great distances beneath the moor, the last of which attempted to link the Pateley Bridge workings to those above Grassington and was about 2,610yd long. The remains of the crushing plant can still be seen on Grassington Moor and are accessible on foot from the end of the road beyond Spring House Farm. Water to drive the plant was scarce and a network of channels which can still be identified across the hillside, brought water over 6 miles from a series of small reservoirs. There is also a remarkable complex of smelt mill flues crossing the moor just below the surface, with a restored terminal stack at the north end.

Limestone pavement above Conistone.

Grass Wood Nature Reserve
B6160 near Grassington
Woodland on limestone habitat.

*Amongst Grassington's old houses is a fruit shop (once a smithy) which housed the notorious Tom Lee who murdered a local doctor and threw the body in the Wharfe. Lee was caught and hanged at York in 1766 and his body afterwards was left on a gibbet near Grass Wood.

Grassington is mostly Georgian in appearance and character, although its foundations are considerably older. The present town grew with the fortunes of nearby lead mining. *Sudden and horrible death features prominently in Grassington's history; it suffered during the Scottish raids of the 14th century and worse by far was the visitation by the Black Death in 1349 which killed a quarter of the inhabitants of the surrounding area. Many villages were wiped out and never recovered; all that is left of once crowded habitations are poignant mounds such as those in Grass Wood, or on the nearby moors. The Upper Wharfedale Museum of farming and industry, together with a fine collection of local minerals, is housed in The Square. Quaint and narrow streets lead off The Square, all lined with interesting buildings. Grassington House is Georgian and the Old Hall, down a side street, has foundations older than are indicated by its venerable facade. Salt Pie Hill, opposite the post office, is where the village stock of salt was kept in the days when salt was the only method of preserving food. Grassington is also the administrative centre for the Yorkshire Dales National Park, the office is on Hebden Road, the B6265.

Footpaths on either bank of the Wharfe above and below Grassington can be linked to give two or three hours' pleasant stroll. A short distance upstream from the road bridge is Ghaistrill's Strid, not quite as dramatic as the one in Bolton Woods downstream, but pretty enough to provide a quiet picnic spot.

A cobbled street in Grassington.

Bank of the Wharfe River Walk – 2 to 3 hours

Upper Wharfedale Museum
Grassington, on B6160 8 miles north-west of Bolton Abbey. Farming and industrial life of Upper Wharfedale.

Although smaller than its neighbour across the valley, **Linton** has the major church in the area. St Michael and All Angels was built in the 14th century and serves the communities of Threshfield, Hebden and Grassington. Linton marks the eastern boundary of the Craven district and certainly the character is changed, with none of the mountainous feel of the Dales, but here a pastoral calm becomes evident with the widening of Craven's broad acres. Linton village, some distance from the church, has a clear stream, a tree-blessed green, a Vanbrughian hospital (almshouse), endowed in 1721 by Richard Fountaine for 'indigent women', and fine houses and cottages built in the 17th and 18th centuries. In a very short distance, Linton Beck is crossed by a clapper bridge, pack-horse bridge, modern road bridge, stepping stones and also a ford, an indication of the once greater importance of this village.

Besom-brooms were once made at **Threshfield**, an industry which was supposed to have been brought to this compact little village by a cattle raiding moss-trooper who became separated from the rest of his gang. Threshfield School is in an attractive Elizabethan building on the Grassington road; Old Pam, a fairy ghost, is supposed to haunt a room above the porch.

Pack-horse bridge, Linton.

Hebden, about two miles downstream from Grassington is mostly built around an ancient stone bridge which was superseded by a larger one built to carry the turnpike, now the B6265 Pateley Bridge road. Hebden village sports are held every August Bank Holiday Monday, fell racing and other athletic events being the main features. A local beauty spot is Scale Force, the approach to which is by a track on the right bank of the stream, leading to the moors.

Above Hebden and along an access road to the north of the B6265, **Grimwith Reservoir** belies its unattractive name. A concessionary footpath from the scenic car park above the dam wall circles the reservoir where wildfowl, especially Canada geese, have made their nesting grounds.

Linton Church.

The glory of **Burnsall** lies in its riverside position and its attractive bridge completes the picture. Built in 1612, it is still strong enough to stand frequent batterings by the Wharfe when in spate. Until this one was built, many bridges had failed the test. The present one is the gift of William Craven, a local boy who made good and became, like Dick Whittington, a Lord Mayor of London. Burnsall is famous for its feast sports which are held on the complicated calendar formulation of the first Saturday after the first Sunday after 12 August. Burnsall's primary school was once an endowed grammar school and was built in 1610. Adjoining it is a church with Anglo-Danish crosses and tombs and a Norse font. Outside are the combined lych-gate and village stocks beside the tree-lined village green.

Above Appletreewick, and by the deeply carved gorge of **Trollers Ghyll** where there is an eerie echo, is **Parcevall Hall**. The Ghyll, or gill is a smaller version of Goredale Scar near Malham. Legend has it that this is where trolls once lived and it is said to be haunted by a phantom dog called Barguest. The beautiful Elizabethan house of Parcevall Hall once sheltered a notorious highwayman by the name of William Nevison who terrorised travellers on nearby roads. The house is now used as a Bradford Diocesan Retreat and Conference Centre. The hall and its beautifully landscaped gardens, are stocked with many rare plants and shrubs.

Parcevall Hall Gardens Skyreholme, near Appletreewick, 10 miles north of Ilkley. Open to the public from Easter to October.

Appletreewick, the locals pronounce it 'Ap'trick', has several fine houses at least 4 - 500 years old, notably High Hall, Monks Hall and Low Hall. High Hall was the home of William Craven. The village was once classed as a township and gained a charter in 1311 to hold a fair which became

Burnsall a popular stopping place on the Wharfe.

known as the 'Onion Fair'. This was abandoned years ago, but Onion Lane is a reminder of that strangely named festival.

The Dales Way follows the river bank all the way down to Bolton Abbey from Grassington. By using the Parklink-Wharfedale bus a full day can be spent walking along what is undoubtedly the finest stretch of the Wharfe.

Almost all the local moors are part of the Duke of Devonshire's Chatsworth estates. Access is permitted to Barden Fell and Barden Moor outside the grouse shooting season and advantage can be taken of this privilege by using access points above Howgill village to get on to Barden Fell. No dogs are allowed and access is withdrawn during times of high fire risk.*

If you are in any doubt about the possibility of shooting going on, or any other problem, it is advisable to contact either the Chatsworth Estate Office or the Yorkshire Dales National Park Information Centre (Tel: Grassington 752774.

Beyond the gently curving right-angled bend opposite Howgill, the Wharfe flows between beech-wooded banks almost as far as Bolton Abbey, and for many this is the most beautiful part of the river. Artists ranging from masters such as Turner to the most amateur, have gained inspiration from its ever changing views.

At Barden Bridge, 17th-century **Barden Tower** fits delightfully into the scene. Now an artist's studio and guest house, the tower was first built by Lord Henry Clifford, the 'Shepherd Lord'; he was known by this title from being brought up by a shepherd's family while a fugitive during the Wars of the Roses. It was he who led the men of Craven at the Battle of Flodden in 1513; the halberd he carried in that battle is still owned by the Clifford family.

Barden Tower
On B6160, 2³/₄ miles north-west of Bolton Abbey.
Artist's study open, art courses held.

Lady Anne Clifford lived most of her younger days at Barden Tower which, like her other properties, was damaged in the Civil War. She was a remarkable lady, for not only did she devote her energies to building and rebuilding but she also did a tremendous amount of philanthropic work in the area. Good works featured not only in Lady Anne Clifford's life; she obviously followed her mother's example who built a hospital at Beamsley, near Bolton Bridge in 1593. The site of the building is away from the village by the side of the A59 and can be recognised from an archway leading into a private garden, but there is now only a circular building remaining of this once extensive structure.

With the exception of the two reservoirs in Barden Beck, **Barden Moor** to the west of Barden Bridge has been granted concessionary access by the Chatsworth estates. Entry points are marked on OS maps and there are the same restrictions as apply to Barden Fell and Simon Seat on the opposite side of the dale.

Below Barden the Wharfe flows through a rocky cleft known as **The Strid**. This deep narrow channel has been worn through softer rock by water action, which has also left strange formations and basins. The Strid means 'stride' but only the foolish attempt to jump the gap. Strategically placed lifebelts should be enough warning, but The Strid has claimed many lives of those who did not heed the sensible advice. Legend has it that a white horse appears whenever someone is about to be drowned in The Strid – so beware if you see one!

Sheepshaw Beck flows down from Hazlewood Moor and through the Valley of Desolation, so named by a topographer who visited the site after a disastrous storm. Woodland again fills the valley where a concessionary footpath leads towards the open moors.

Footpaths follow both banks of the Wharfe into **Bolton Woods**. Those on the west bank were established between 1789 and 1843 by the vicar of Bolton Priory church, the Reverend William Carr. He began a tradition of public access which has continued to the present time. The first visitors came from mill towns of the West Riding, by train to the now abandoned Bolton Abbey Station and then by wagonette to the priory and Strid Wood. For people who normally worked a 50 to 60 hour week this place would be like heaven. The woods are part of the Chatsworth estates and a small charge is made towards upkeep of the paths. This is payable at the Strid Cottage entrance or the Cavendish Pavilion. Five nature trails are

> **The Strid and Bolton Woods**
> Access from B6160.
> Deep narrow gorge with water-worn formations. Nature trails.
> Small fee.

Parcevall Hall, Wharfedale.

Bolton Abbey
A59. 6¹/₂ miles east of Skipton. Ruined Augustinian priory.

Richard Moon, the last prior, tried to save Bolton Abbey from dissolution by a bribe of £10 sent to Thomas Cromwell, Henry VIII's lieutenant, but this had no effect and the monks were driven out into the world on 29 January 1540. The abbey soon fell into ruins, its stones used in local buildings, but the nave was spared and became the parish church.

laid out in the woods and an explanatory booklet is on sale. Wheelchair access is available to most of the abbey grounds, riverside and woodland walks, including the Strid viewpoint.

The soaring ruined arch of **Bolton Abbey's** east window which dominates the wide sweep of the River Wharfe, is the result of the Dissolution by Henry VIII in 1540. Until then it had been home for a small community of Augustinian canons since 1154. Obeying a life of chastity and poverty, the monks, or more correctly Black Canons, came to this delightful spot after living for 34 years at nearby Embsay. Each wore a black cassock and a sleeved surplice with a hooded cloak fastened only at the neck; a black square cap covered their heads. Even though the order prospered from extensive lead mining and wool interests, the monks spent most of their days in prayer, or looking after the needs of the local people. Life, however was not always tranquil; in 1318 and 1320 Black Douglas, a Scottish border raider, twice attacked Bolton Abbey during forays into Craven. Strictly it is not an abbey but a priory. However, Bolton Abbey is the most commonly used title, a name which has also been given to the nearby village.* Standing on a high wooded promontory above the abbey, the ornate six-sided Cavendish Memorial Fountain was built in memory of Lord Frederick Charles Cavendish, second son of the 7th Duke of Devonshire, who was assassinated in Phoenix Park, Dublin in 1882.

Crossing the busy A59 at Bolton Bridge and moving downstream by the B6160, one enters ever increasing urbanisation, but the towns of mid-Wharfedale still retain their Dales' character. **Addingham**, once a double line of cottages along what became the A65, dates from Anglian times and is named after a local chieftain 'Adda'. The church still embodies many of its original Norman features, especially a number of its arches. The town developed during the 18th century around five water mills. Four of them were textile mills and no longer function, but the fifth, a timber mill, still operates. One of the textile mills was attacked by Luddites during unrest in the early part of the Industrial Revolution.

Ilkley, the start of the Dales Way, was *Olicana* to the Romans who built a fort there, but little remains except that the site is known and two Roman altars have been built into the basement of the church tower. Ilkley parish church has foundations which go back to the dawn of Christianity in the Dales;

Bolton Abbey.

three Runic crosses stand in the churchyard and in the wall of the south aisle the recumbent cross-legged statue of Sir Adam de Myddleton has lain there since his death in 1315. Adjacent to the church is the Elizabethan manor house, now a museum, which was built on the site of the fort's west gate. Modern Ilkley developed first with pretentions of being a spa town and later along with neighbouring Otley it became a dormitory for the wool kings of Leeds and Bradford. With its back to Rombalds Moor (known throughout the country as Ilkley Moor) and the setting of Yorkshire's 'national anthem' – On Ilkla Moor Baht'at – Ilkley is a fine place to live. Few towns of its size can boast so much open country opening from the top of their High Street.*

Below the outcrop of Ilkley Crags a solitary building marks the site of '**White Wells**', an 18th-century bath house built by a local benefactor. A walk from the Cow and Calf along the edge of the moor will take in all these features. Another popular Ilkley Moor walk is across to the famous Dick Hudson's pub above Shipley.

The Wharfe flows eastwards away from the Dales, but fortunately misses the industrial heartland of Yorkshire. Beyond Ilkley the river passes its sister town of Otley which was granted a market charter in 1222. The river continues, round the northern boundary of Yorkshire's major house, Harewood, to skirt the racecourse town of Wetherby and on into the Vale of York, past Samuel Smith's brewery at Tadcaster to join the Ouse and eventually the sea.

*Visitors to Ilkley can hardly avoid seeing the distinctive mass of the Cow and Calf rocks. Behind them the moor is rich in the carved stones of our prehistoric ancestors who have left not only their cairns and circles but enigmatically carved 'cup-and-ring' stones and the famous Swastika Stone above Heber's Ghyll. This was supposedly the symbol of fire worship and one of only three in the world, the others being in Greece and Sweden.

White Wells
Ilkley Moor
Private house, but arrangements can be made to view the history and geology display.

Airedale

On first sight it would seem that the River Aire starts its life as the stream issuing from the letterbox shaped hole at the foot of Malham Cove. However it is in a direct line below Malham Tarn, which undoubtedly is the true parent of industrial Yorkshire's major river.

Dalescape above Airedale.

Malham Cove.

*The Aire has not always flowed below ground and at one time a waterfall higher than Niagara poured over the lip of Malham Cove. Local records seem to indicate that the fall dried up some time in the late 18th century, although there is no factual proof of this.

Nature has arranged for a complicated switch to occur out of site and below ground. The stream flowing from Malham Tarn disappears underground at Water Sinks immediately south of the tarn, only to reappear as the quiet spring known as Aire Head about half a mile south of Malham Village. The stream issuing from the foot of Malham Cove started as an insignificant pair of runnels west of the Littondale road.*

It is strange to find surface water, and especially a lake, in limestone country. The reason for it is that patches of Silurian slate, which is impervious to water, occur throughout Craven and the particular patch above Malham holds this tarn. Other examples of this slate can be found at a considerably lower level around Horton in the Ribble Valley. Although of the same geological age, the reason for such a marked shift is due to a massive downward movement of the earth's crust, known here as the 'Mid-Craven Fault'. The actual fracture can be traced by the line of dramatic cliffs including Malham Cove and Attermire Scar above Settle.

Beef cattle graze Malham Moor, but it is sheep which provide the real income to the area. They have been the mainstay for hundreds of years, from the early times and later when huge flocks roamed the fells, building the fortunes of Fountains Abbey. This monastery owned most of the land in the surrounding district, but Fountains Fell is the only tangible link with an order which prospered until the Dissolution.

Airedale

Malham Tarn, a rarity in a limestone region.

Malham Tarn
2 miles north of Malham.
Moorland lake,
bird/nature sanctuary.
Refreshments, car
parking and information
centre available in
Malham.

*Charles Kingsley stayed at Malham Tarn House and was so inspired by the scenery that he made it the backcloth of his novel The Water Babies. He also used the magical aspect of the mysterious pool at the foot of Malham Cove, which became the place where the water babies made their home.

While Fountains Fell is made of gritstone and grows a plentiful but sour grass, the land to the east of the upland farm , Tennant Gill, stands on limestone. Here the grass is much shorter, but sweeter. Limestone makes the whole long complex line of summits running east towards **Kilnsey Moor** as a maze of outcrops and boulders. This is a fascinating area for the birdwatcher or botanist, and especially the fossil hunter. The land is almost free of visitors so be careful not to break a bone on the often slippery limestone. A few public footpaths, which can be followed by careful navigation, cross the heights between Malham Moor and Littondale.

Malham Tarn and its surrounds are owned by the National Trust and the estate has been devoted to the study of flora and fauna of the area. Malham Tarn House is used as a centre by the Field Studies Council and courses are held for a variety of student bodies. Once a shooting lodge, the present use for the preservation of wildlife has encouraged an increase in the bird population, especially wild fowl which visit the lake during their nesting season.

By using two quiet stretches of road round Tarn Moss, and then a footpath, Malham Tarn can be circumnavigated in a couple of hours, but it is a fair bet that the walker's footsteps will be slow along the side of the tarn, especially in spring when the birds congregate and begin their courtship rituals.*

During the formative years of the world, tremendous upheavals took place and today it will be difficult to imagine the cataclysmic earthquakes which rent the face of the earth and reversed the relative heights of land in the Craven area. Nowhere along the Mid-Craven Fault is this so evident as at Malham. Land at the foot of **Malham Cove** started on the same level as the summit of Fountains Fell with the cove marking the fracture line of the fault. On top of Malham

Malham Cove, one of the Yorkshire Dales' major attractions.

Malham Cove
½ mile north of Malham. Limestone amphitheatre with water-worn pavement on higher level.

Cove is a remarkable limestone pavement, a wide expanse of clefts in the bare rock made by the action of water working its way down through weaker sections of this soluble rock. The clefts or 'grikes' are filled with varieties of ferns such as hart's tongue fern and dog's mercury; plants normally living in shaded woodland and associated with the ground cover of ash woodland which covered most of the fells before the last Ice Age. The flat parts between the grikes are known as 'clints'.

In a field below the cove, ruined walls at right angles to the path are themselves prehistoric and were built by the first men who settled in this sheltered and fertile little valley. Lynchets on either side of the valley beneath the cove and clapper bridges across the beck also speak of man's long occupation of this sunny place. Despite being one of the most popular villages in the dales, **Malham** retains an unhurried rural charm. The Yorkshire Dales National Park Authority are to be congratulated on the way they have resisted attempts to commercialise Malham, and yet at the same time the village caters admirably for the needs of visitors. Malham is a very nice place in which to live as well as visit - not an easy combination to achieve.

The National Park Authority has provided a large car park and a very useful information centre on the edge of Malham village. Malham has attracted visitors for many years. Wordsworth and his sister Dorothy spent some time in the area in 1807 and the line 'Where young lions crouch' composed after the visit, aptly sums up the feel

Gordale Scar ravine was once a cavern.

of the crags and precipices of the cove and its neighbours. Malham has many more visitors than it did before the bridge by the green was widened. This was necessary to cope with motors rather than pack-horse traffic for which it was first built. Even older than this is Moon Bridge, an ancient clapper bridge a little way upstream by the side of Beck Hall, where on a sunny day the attraction of the river and cream teas can be irresistible.

The pack-horse road which crossed Malhamdale can still be followed most of its way on footpaths or by a little-used road. This is the route which climbs out from Settle by way of Attermire Scar and crosses Kirkby Fell by Nappa Cross before calling in on Malham. Next it crosses the bridge and climbs to Gordale and steeply back to the moors, where it becomes Mastiles Lane and so eventually down into Wharfedale by the side of Kilnsey Crag.

Lead was mined above Malham but the only visible remnant (except for the occasional blanked off shaft here and there) is the lonely chimney to the right of the Littondale road – all that survives of the smelt mill for the area. Mining of a different kind went on below Pikedaw Hill, west of Malham, where zinc in the form of calamine (zinc carbonate) was extracted from below ground.

About a mile north-east from Malham, along the road towards Mastiles Lane, is the breathtaking spectacle of

Gordale Scar. Here a collapsed cave system has formed a narrow gorge with towering and overhanging cliffs on either side. Most visitors will not care to emulate the rock gymnasts performing over their heads and in fact most people turn back at the point where the waterfall rushes down its tufa buttress. Tufa is rock which is made from deposits of limestone held in suspension in the stream; as the water flows over existing rocks it leaves behind minute amounts of lime to form a porous 'reconstituted' stone. Footholds on the buttress to the left of the waterfall make it easier to climb than first impressions might show and in fact the scree slope above is probably more difficult to any-one wearing foorwear other than boots. To the walker's right of the scree slope the river pours though a natural window in the rock wall.

> **Gordale Scar**
> 1¹/₂ miles east of Malham.
> Deep limestone gorge formed by a collapsed cave system.

Below Gordale Scar and across the road the river tumbles over another tufa outcrop. This one, known as **Janet's Foss**, is a perfect gem set amongst shady trees and mossy rocks. Standing by it on a sunny day it is easy to believe the local legend that Janet, a fairy queen, lives behind the outcrop.

> **Janet's Foss**
> 1 mile East of Malham. Cascade over a moss-grown tufa block at the bottom of a wooded dell. Nature trail.

The Pennine Way which has followed the Aire from Eshton Moor and through Malham village, climbs the cove, but instead of following the interesting dry valley above it, takes a parallel course along Trougate to the Tarn. Beyond, the route is semi-artificial, wandering through fields to Tennant Gill and then up to Fountains Fell and across the intervening col to Pen-y-ghent hill.

After the dramatic scenery around Malham, the char-acter of Airedale quickly changes to the lush pasture which has made Craven's dairy farms so famous. On either side of the river are two ancient villages. **Hanlith** to the east was founded by the Saxons, and its hall built in 1668 retains a Jacobean flavour despite later alter-ations. Westwards is the upper valley's main village, **Kirkby Malham**, where the dale's first church (St Michael the Archangel) was founded in the 8th century. Outside it is a preaching cross and a set of stocks which look as though they could still be put into use today.*

*Oliver Cromwell is supposed to have witnessed three marriages in Kirkby Malham's church and there is a signature which looks like his on the register, but there is nothing else to authen-ticate his visit to this valley during the long and bitter northern campaign in the Civil War.

The next two villages almost mirror their upstream neighbours in their positions east and west of the river. **Calton** is on the hilltop to the east and was home for 'Honest' John Lambert, one of Cromwell's generals. **Airton** is linked more closely to the river, which once powered the former linen mill, now converted into flats.

Skipton marina on the Leeds-Liverpool canal.

Leeds-Liverpool Canal
Open to pleasure craft. Boat hire from Gargrave and Skipton. Busy set of locks near Malham road on outskirts of Gargrave.

Foulridge Canal Cruises
Canal Wharf Foulridge, Colne. The 'Marton Emperor' offers a one and a half hour cruise along the Leeds-Liverpool Canal.

Airton was a Quaker stronghold and still holds links with this gentle faith.

Strategically placed in the Aire Gap, **Gargrave** straddles the A65 as well as being served by the railway and a canal. Transport throughout the ages has passed through this village. Prehistoric man used the Aire Gap to cross the Pennines on an established trade route between Ireland and Scandinavia, and the Romans followed by building a road from Ribchester to link in with their main north-south arteries on either side of York. A battle associated with the legend of King Arthur is supposed to have taken place somewhere in this gap through the Pennines, but its site is unknown.

As the Yorkshire wool trade developed, improvements to the roads between the sheep-rearing areas and factory towns followed. In 1753 the turnpiking of the Keighley to Kendal road made it much easier for wool to be brought from Westmorland to industrial West Riding. A few years later waterways were promoted which were intended to link Liverpool with the east coast at Hull. In 1770 an Act of Parliament authorised the building of a canal between Liverpool and Leeds. Work progressed rapidly on the lower stretches, but it was not until 1790 that the full length was opened, with the completion of the difficult stretch on either side of Gargrave. Canals fell into disuse with the advent of railways, and by 1876 the Leeds to Carlisle railway was in operation.

Gargrave's bridge over the Aire.

Today motor traffic speeds through Gargrave on surfaces far smoother than the builders of the turnpike ever envisaged. The railway is still open, but is frequently the cause of commercial headshaking in sections of rail management. The canal, which has not carried any commercial traffic since 1954, has benefited with the increasing popularity of canal cruising. During the holiday season the locks around Gargrave are in almost constant use as pleasure craft climb up to Craven and down to Skipton. Throughout the centuries Gargrave has seen a great deal of traffic of one kind or another. Traffic has not always been friendly though. The Roman villa south-east of the village was found, during recent excavations, to have been sacked in the 3rd century. The site of the villa is on private land, but can be seen from the lane running from the side of the church towards the railway line. The Scots also created much mayhem when they visited Gargrave in 1318 on a cattle raiding excursion. Walkers enjoying one of the most pastoral sections of the Pennine Way, pass through Gargrave on their way to Malham and the limestone regions of the Pennines.

Side valleys in the Dales often lead to pleasant surprises for those who try to avoid the more crowded places. When, as often happens, Malham is overcrowded and the traffic crawls through Skipton, the little **Winterburn Valley** above Gargrave will provide a haven of peace and quiet. Few roads and pathways traverse this valley but those that do are worth following. No villages occupy the main valley but its tributary gives anchorage to three which are very close together. Cracoe is the first, most industrialised and providing homes for quarry workers and lorry drivers, but **Hetton** and **Rylstone** are more attractive places. **Rylstone Fell** to the east provides some excellent walking and good rock climbing on the gritstone edge of the moor. Being part of the Chatsworth estate, concessionary access has been granted to the fell except during grouse shooting or at times of high fire risk.

Craven is shaped roughly like an inverted south-west pointing 'V', with agriculture gradually giving way to industry the closer one gets to Lancashire, but even so there is still much delightful and unspoilt countryside to find. East of Thornton-in-Craven the gentle heights of Pinhaw Beacon and neighbouring Kelbrook Moor are a blaze of purple heather in August and September during the grouse shooting season. Heather, being the staple diet of grouse, is encouraged, and so there is the side benefit of a wealth of rich colour in late summer.

Earby never quite succumbed to the growth of industry as did the other cotton towns further south beneath the slopes of Pendle Hill. Elizabethan stone houses can still be found in odd corners, often alongside modern factories. One such building, the 17th-century grammar school, has been preserved as a lead mining museum by the Earby Mines Research Group. The collection of mining mementoes ranges from clogs and miner's hats, to working models and a unique ore crusher from Providence Mine near Kettlewell. As it is run by a voluntary society the museum's opening times are restricted.

> **Earby Museum of Mines**
> Earby A56, 6 miles south-west of Skipton. Large collection of Yorkshire Dales' mining equipment, working models, mineral samples, etc. Limited opening.

On the edge of Lancashire's cotton domain and a mile or two outside Colne is the unique living museum of **Wycoller**, a village which started life over eleven centuries ago as a hill settlement, and in the 18th and 19th centuries enjoyed a mini-boom as an industrial hamlet. This boom was short lived, as it was based on handloom weaving, and with the advent of mechanical power industry moved to the more open spaces of Colne and the Calder Valley. Wycoller Hall was used by Charlotte Brontë as Ferndean Manor in her novel *Jane Eyre*. Slowly the hall and village fell into decay until 1950, when the Friends of Wycoller came into existence and the decay was halted. But it took until 1973 to bring about any true preservation, when the area was designated a Country Park and Conservation Area. Apart from

> **Wycoller Country Park**
> Off Haworth road 3 miles from Colne.

providing a small visitor information service and generally tidying up the ruins and paths, the authorities have had the foresight to leave Wycoller for the visitor to explore and discover its delightful facets. Car parking is kept outside the village and one must walk in to enjoy the area. Several paths follow the valley as far as the Haworth road and there are numerous permutations on a theme to provide round trips for walkers.

Moving back into Yorkshire along the A6068 towards Airedale, the industrial township of **Cowling** and its satellite Ickornshaw hold a tenacious foothold to the industrial 20th century. The moors south of the road are sour and with little interest, but **Earl Crag** is worth visiting if only to view the curious towers known respectively as Wainman's Pinnacle and Lund's Tower.

Sheltering beneath the bulk of Elslack Moor is **Lothersdale**, a village of quaint and interesting houses, which manages the almost impossible task of remaining relatively prosperous without losing any of its character. The woollen mill provides work for most of the inhabitants of Lothersdale, and still retains its waterwheel although power is now from the more modern and reliable source of electricity. Persecuted Quakers sheltered here during the reign of King Charles II; their quaint Meeting House, with its peep-hatch gallery is still used. Charlotte Brontë used Stone Gappe, the attractive Georgian house to the east of the village, for Gateshead Hall in *Jane Eyre*.

The most southerly of Yorkshire's lead mining districts and by chance the last to be developed is between Lothersdale and Cononley. Here a single but rich vein occurs beneath a gritstone layer. While lead had been mined for centuries around this district, it was not until 1830 that serious development took place, producing some 150,000 tons of ore in the period up to 1876. The engine house and smelt mill chimney are still in very good condition and have been preserved in a joint venture by the Earby Mines Research Group and the Crosshills Naturalist Society.

Dales and industry both meet and co-exist in **Skipton,** where miles of sewing cotton are produced. The Dales' farmer and his wife come down to market to shop alongside visitors out for the day from nearby towns and

Skipton Castle
11th-century, restored by Lady Anne Clifford between 1650-75 and still in excellent repair. Open to the public.

Skipton Castle stands at the head of Skipton's busy market street.

In 1138 William Fitzduncan, nephew of King David I of Scotland, attacked Skipton castle but he was then conquered by Alice de Romille whom he married in 1152. Peace reigned over Skipton for several centuries during which the Clifford family took over the castle as protectors against the Scots. In 1642, during the ownership of the indefatigable Lady Anne Clifford, the castle was held by Sir John Mallory and 300 men for three years against Cromwell's troops. Starvation eventually forced their surrender on 21 December 1645. Lady Anne could not return to her castle until 1650 and it took the next 25 years until her death in 1675, to rebuild the castle to its present appearance.

Other places to visit around Skipton

Craven Museum
Situated in High Street close to the castle, exhibiting a collection of Craven mementoes. Open most afternoons.

High Corn Mill
Mill Bridge
Still producing corn by the power of two waterwheels. Open to the public.

cities. Good wholesome food is traditionally offered by the many inns lining, or not far from, the High Street. Skipton has long been a major market town at the crossroads of routes justifying its claim to be the 'Gateway to the Dales'. Certainly it is ideally situated as a tourist centre, especially since new by-pass roads were built, removing the frequent snarl-ups in the High Street. The town was established long before the Normans built a castle here and recorded the name 'Sceptone' or 'Sheeptown'. The *Domesday Book* lists the land around Skipton as Crown land which was later granted to Robert de Romille.*

The imposing gateway to the castle with its Clifford motto 'Desormais', roughly meaning 'Henseforth' is a lasting memorial to Lady Anne's work. The castle is a private house, but open to the public for most of the year.

An exhibition of life in Old Craven is on show in the Craven Museum in Skipton town hall below the castle, together with relics of the three-year siege during the Civil War and even older finds. A 'living' museum can be found nearby at High Corn Mill on Ellerbeck where flour is still produced by power generated by two waterwheels. The mill is as old as the town, one on the same site having been mentioned in the Domesday Book. Skipton parish church watches over the comings and goings at the top of the market street. Though greatly 'improved' in the Victorian era, much of the fabric dates from 17th-century restoration by Lady Anne Clifford, after the severe damage it sustained along with the adjoining castle during the Civil War.

The Springs branch of the **Leeds-Liverpool Canal** ends in Skipton at a busy basin; its almost constant movement of pleasure craft is only a short distance from the market. Skipton has its own 'private' moor to the east of the town where a network of paths remain from the time when people from the remote farm houses scattered over the moor, walked to and from Skipton to sell their produce at the market. **Embsay** is on the A59, two miles outside Skipton, the headquarters of the **Yorkshire Dales Railway Society** who have preserved a section of the old Ilkley to Skipton line. Lack of line has not deterred the society from collecting a large number of locomotives and rolling stock which are steamed regularly, especially at summer and Bank Holiday weekends.

Ever-increasing industrial towns line the Aire and the clear waters of Malhamdale are more and more polluted as the river approaches Leeds. High to the east is

Rombald's Moor and as previously seen in the chapter on Wharfedale, even though many tracks cross the moor from one valley to the other, few paths actually go round. However it is possible to walk from Silsden to Riddlesden on recognised rights-of-way.

Kildwick is the last true 'Dales' village in Airedale, an ancient place founded by the Saxons who named it 'Childwic'. The church, often referred to as the Lang Kirk of Craven, is 176ft long, one of the longest in Yorkshire. The present building is 16th-century, but its foundations are much older. Another old Kildwick structure is the much altered bridge across the Aire, which dates from the 14th century. The imposing manor house is Elizabethan, now tastefully converted into an hotel and restaurant and for 300 years was the home of the Currer family.

On no account should **Keighley** be written off as just another industrial town. Its art gallery in Cliffe Castle is worth visiting, as is its modern town centre, if only to see the Neolithic 'cup-and-ring' stone, uprooted from its true place on the moors to make an unusual town centre feature. Just outside Keighley on the Bradford road is **East Riddlesden Hall**, built in 1642, which boasts a magnificent banqueting hall and one of the finest timbered barns in the north of England.

In 1867 a railway line was opened to link the industrial mill towns of the Worth Valley to the main line at Keighley. This branch line continued to serve the scattered communities of the valley until 1962 when it was no longer considered an economical proposition. With the growth of nostalgic interest in steam engines it was a heaven sent opportunity. Members of the Keighley and Worth Valley Railway Preservation Society banded together for the specific purpose of bringing the line back to life and especially to run it as a commercial venture by using steam locomotives. A great deal of work was necessary both to bring the line and rolling stock up to the high standards required by the Ministry of Transport and more importantly, to raise the necessary cash to fund the venture. Money was needed not only to purchase the line, but also to buy the right to use Platform 4 on Keighley station. At 2.35pm on Saturday 29 June 1968 the hopes and ambitions of all the many people who had worked towards re-opening the line were realised, when a beflagged train, drawn by two locomotives pulled away from Keighley station. Since then the society has run

Keighley
East Riddlesden Hall
On A650, 1 mile north-east of Keighley. Manor house and great barn. National Trust.

Brontë weaving Shed
Keighley. Edinburgh Woollen Mill collections. Fully operating water wheel.

Cup-and-Ring Stone
Centre piece of Keighley market place. Prehistoric symbolic carving uprooted from nearby moorland.

Keighley and Worth Valley Railway
Steam railway from Keighley BR Station to Oxenhope.

Haworth
Brontë Parsonage and Museum. Memorabilia of the Brontë family, paintings, manuscripts, costumes, etc.

Scartop Pine Village
Moor Lodge, Stanbury, Worth Valley. The converted gentleman's shooting lodge provides a nostalgic trip through Victorian room settings.

Penistone Hill Country Park
¹/₂ mile south-west of Haworth.

**Wuthering Heights Walk
4 miles – 2 hours**

In Wuthering Heights Emily Brontë enlarged the building of Top Withins Farm but on a wild and foggy day late in the year, it is not difficult to people it with the ghosts of Catherine and Heathcliff.

steam trains every Saturday, Sunday and Bank Holidays and on certain weekdays in summer. The whole venture continues to be operated by enthusiastic volunteers and the profits are ploughed back to help buy new rolling stock and maintain the line. The full range of equipment is fully preserved and on view in the station yards of Haworth and Oxenhope.*

A trip on the Worth Valley Line can be included in a visit to **Haworth**, if only as a pilgrimage to the parsonage home of the Brontë sisters, daughters of the Reverend Patrick Brontë who was minister of Haworth's Church of St Michael and All Angels. Here is where Anne, Charlotte and Emily wrote their novels, set so often amongst local buildings and places. Even without its links with the Brontës, Haworth would be worth visiting if only for its evocative atmosphere which recalls the 19th century; from its cobbled Main Street to the gritstone houses laid out in a planner's nightmare. One must however forgive the slight air of commercialism which has made traders link the name of Brontë to almost every saleable item; they have a living to make after all.

Penistone Hill above the village has been made into a Country Park and is ideally situated for picnics, or gentle wandering along the edge of the moors. In late summer the sheer enjoyment of the acres of heather recalls the love Yorkshire composer Delius had for the rolling moors and open skies of his native county. This is the sunny view of Yorkshire, rather than the sullen impetuousness of the Brontë sisters, more fitted to a wild stormy day when the dripping clouds cover everything.

A walk that Brontë devotees will follow is the one to **Top Withins Farm**, or Wuthering Heights. The farm, now a ruin, is a typical hill farm made uneconomical when reservoirs were built on good valley bottom land.* The path to Top Withins starts at the cross roads between the Country Park and Lower Laithe Reservoir.

The Pennine Way route passes Top Withins and two miles further on is **Ponden Hall**, also with Brontë associations. This house is reputed to be Thrushcross Grange in *Wuthering Heights*. The building has been preserved with a lot of care and attention given to the spacious rooms, with their massive oak beams and wide stone fireplaces. Pennine Way walkers and seekers of Brontë lore can all enjoy Ponden as its main use today is to provide food and accommodation.

Following the Pennine Way southwards the route crosses the watershed from the Aire into the last of the mid-Pennine valleys, the Calder. Although no longer Dales' country and heavily industrialised around the actual river, the **Calder Valley** offers an amazing variety of lonely moors, deep wooded valleys and unspoilt villages with a heritage which seems to have remained almost unaltered since the 18th century. Then, industrialisation meant handloom weaving in tiny cottages; cottages which are still identifiable by the rows of windows in their attic rooms.

A pack-horse trail crossed Widdop Moor from Burnley to Halifax and a tiny inn on the Hebden Bridge to Colne road offered shelter. Below the Pack Horse Inn, Hebden Water leads down to a lovely wooded valley. In it Hardcastle Crags have, on occasions, served as the setting for the traditional open-air parliament for Swiss nationals living in Britain. **Hebden Bridge**, with its terraced cottages appearing to defy gravity, makes an ideal centre for Calderdale, or perhaps the visitor will stray to Heptonstall high on its hillside. **Heptonstall**, with its Easter Pace Egg competitions, is one of Yorkshire's most rewarding villages for visitors interested in the history of the domestic weaving trade. Across the valley is **Mankinholes**, dominated by the obelisk on Stoodley Pike, erected to commemorate the defeat of Napoleon in 1814. It has collapsed twice and been restored each time.

A long distance path known as the Calderdale Way roughly follows the watershed of all the tributaries of the Calder. It visits many fascinating places and crosses quiet moors and offers 50 miles of interesting walking which can be easily split into seven days splendid walking.

Calder Valley Cruising
Barge Branwell
The Marina, Hebden Bridge.
Horse drawn traditional canal barge. Lunch and tea cruises a speciality. From Easter to Christmas.

Calderdale Way
50 miles – 7 days

Limestone pavement, Malham Cove.

Selected Walks

Maps

The Ordnance Survey maps which cover the area of this book are: Touring Map and Guide to the Yorkshire Dales; 1 inch to one mile. 1:50,000 Landranger Series, sheets 87, 90, 91, 92, 97, 98, 99, 102, 103, 104, 110: 1:25,000 Outdoor Leisure Series, The Three Peaks, Malham and Upper Wharfedale, South Pennines and Teesdale. Harveys Superwalker Map – the Howgill covers this corner of the Dales.

Rights-of-Way

A number of walks described in this book are across open moors or limestone pavements. Although in some instances official rights-of-way do not exist, all the routes have been walked for many years by countless people without hindrance, are still regularly used and feature in most local guidebooks. It is hoped that in the near future formal agreements can be arranged for free access.

Cycling in the Yorkshire Dales

The Dales are criss-crossed with hundreds of miles of quiet side roads suitable for cyclists of all levels, from family groups to the most experienced. The 2 miles to 1 inch Yorkshire Dales Cycling Map in the 'Goldeneye' Series, gives a comprehensive selection of routes, many of which may be joined to make longer rides.

Ribblesdale (p.20)

Attermire Scar
5 miles – moderate to strenuous – 2³/₄ hours

The walk starts from Settle, 'capital' of Upper Ribblesdale. Follow the road left of the market place towards Constitution Hill. Bear right along a rough walled lane as far as a stile and turn right. Climb to a clump of trees and turn right along a path signposted to Malham. Cross the grassy hillside, go over two stiles and through a gap in a wall. Turn left to follow a path beneath Attermire Scar and past a series of shallow caves where prehistoric and post-Roman remains were found. Climb up to a metal gate and go left down a well-made farm lane. Where the lane is about to join a road, turn left through a small gate to follow a field path along the bottom edge of a mature wood. Go between two sections of woodland and walk down a path into the outskirts of Settle.

Catrigg and Stainforth Force
5 miles – Moderate – 2³/₄ hours

Visiting two attractive waterfalls makes this an ideal walk for a hot day. From the roadside car park in Stainforth walk as far as the Craven Heifer Inn, then follow the lane opposite as far as a tiny green surrounding a group of stone cottages. Turn right to climb a walled lane marked 'Unsuitable for Motors'. At a gate marking the top of the lane, climb the stile on the left to go down to Catrigg Force; return to the gate to continue the walk. Cross a stile next to the gate and turn right, uphill across an open field. Cross another stile, turn right as directed by a signpost to Winskill Farm. Do not enter the farmyard, but keep ahead through a gate and downhill on a track signposted to Langcliffe. Climb over a ladder stile on the left and walk downhill through rocky fields, then into a belt of gnarled trees. Go through a small gate and, keeping above an old quarry, cross three fields to reach Langcliffe. Bear right at the village green and walk down to the main road. Turn right as far as a railway bridge then turn left down a lane to a group of riverside cottages. Cross the river by a footbridge and turn right, upstream following the riverbank as far as Stainforth Force and its pack-horse bridge. Turn at the bridge and follow the lane to the main road: Stainforth village is ¹/₄ mile to the right.

Stainforth Bridge.

A riverside walk from Horton-in-Ribblesdale – 5 miles – easy – 2 hours

From the car park, walk to the footbridge and turn right, downstream. Following signposts walk along the riverbank for a little over a mile to a footbridge. Cross the bridge and bear left uphill over a series of fields, crossing boundary walls by their stiles. At the road turn left then right at a barn beside a loop road. Follow the signpost's direction over the fields at Dub Cote Farm. Go down to a minor road and turn right into the outskirts of Horton. Cross the stream by a footbridge on your right and follow a lane signposted 'Pennine Way' as far as a lane junction. Turn left, downhill into Horton where the car park is to the right, but perhaps more important, the Three Peaks Café is even closer.

Lune Valley (p.40)

Ingleton's Waterfalls
4¹/₂ miles – moderate/slippery areas after rain – 2¹/₂ hours

Probably the most beautiful walk in the Yorkshire Dales, the fact that a small toll is charged does not detract from its interest. Amateur geologists will find evidence of the complex history of the underlying strata of the district; non geologists can follow the short informative guide to the Ingleton Waterfalls Trail produced by the Yorkshire Dales National Park.

From the car park follow the footpath upstream through Swilla Glen, passing Pecca Falls and Thornton Force (snack-bar nearby). Climb out on to the open pasture and cross a footbridge. Turn right along a narrow lane past Twistleton Hall, then by footpath to Beezleys Farm (refreshments). Follow a signposted path downhill into the narrowing valley to pass Beezley and Snow Falls. Where the angle of descent improves a track leads on towards Ingleton Church; the car park is below on the right.

Pecca Falls, Ingleton.

Dentdale
6 miles – moderate – 4 hours

This walk explores Dentdale upstream from the unspoilt village of Dent. Walk along Dent's cobbled streets, past the church towards Church Bridge. Do not cross the river, but turn right following a side stream, Keld Beck, as far as a farmhouse. Keep ahead at the farm to reach a gravel path leading up the road at Bridge End. Cross the road and follow a signposted woodland path out to open fields. On sighting a ruined farmhouse, bear left towards the Deepdale Beck following stiles marking the way. At a stone barn, go left across a footbridge and walk downstream a little way, then bear right up a leafy lane into a farmyard. Turn right through the yard and along a lane. Turn sharp left at a low stone building and climb a steep bank leading to a stile; cross this and walk towards Rigg End Farm. Cross the access drive and bear left in front of the farm, aiming for a line of trees. Go past the trees, down through open fields and join the lane at a ruined barn. Turn right along the lane then right again at the road. Go past Whernside Manor then left, along a footpath signposted to Tommy Bridge; cross the bridge and turn left. downstream; right at a sign pointing to a shady path, then left on reaching the valley road. Follow the road to Tommy Bridge, then into Dent village.

Sedgwick Memorial, Dent.

Winder Hill
4¹/₂ miles – strenuous – 3 hours

To climb this attractive little hill overlooking Sedbergh, walk along High Street, past the church then turn right into Howgill Lane, following it as far as the

30mph limit. Turn right along a farm lane signposted 'To the Fell'. Go half right through Lockbank farmyard, then left by a grassy path alongside a boundary wall and past a pine wood. Turn right steeply uphill to climb across Winder's summit, go down to a broad col and turn right on a well defined path leading back to Lockbank Farm. Do not enter the farmyard, but turn left away from the farm, following the boundary wall as far as a kissing gate. Turn right and go through the gate and walk downhill beside a shaley gorge. Join a farm lane, following it into the outskirts of Sedbergh; the church and central car park are on the right as you enter the town.

North Pennines (p.58)

The South Tyne
4¹/₂ miles – Easy – 2 hours

This is an easy walk to follow, down one bank of the South Tyne and up the other! Part of the route uses one of the prettiest sections of the Pennine Way to the north of Garrigill, a charming ex-lead mining village.

From the George and Dragon in Garrigill, follow Pennine Way signs downstream, first along a road then by fieldpath and through a narrow strip of beechwood on the west bank of the river. Ignoring a signposted footbridge taking the Pennine Way across the river continue downstream to the confluence of the South Tyne and Black Burn. Cross the main river at this point and climb up to Bleagate Farm; turn right on a path leading upstream. Go past Sillyhall Farm and into woodland, again ignoring the Pennine Way bridge to walk upstream through the trees and join a minor road by the corner of a cemetery. Turn right and follow this road into Garrigill.

Teesdale (p.76)

Cauldron Snout
9¹/₂ miles – fairly strenuous – 5 hours

The walk to this dramatic waterfall is from Langdon Beck Youth Hostel on the B6277 road through Teesdale. Follow Pennine Way signs opposite the hostel and along a farm lane to Saur Hill Farm. Continue by footpath down to the Tees and follow it, upstream.

At Falcon Clints the going is quite rocky, leading to the dramatic spectacle of Cauldron Snout. Climb the rocks at the side of the waterfall with care, especially after rain when they can be exceptionally slippery. Follow the access road to your right of Cow Green Reservoir and across Widdybank Fell. Continue along the road until you reach a road bridge over Harwood Beck; do not cross the bridge, but turn right downstream to Saur Hill and go left over the bridge to reach the Youth Hostel.

Low Force and High Force
4 miles – easy – 1³/₄ hours

Visiting two contrasting waterfalls, the walk follows part of the Teesdale section of the Pennine Way. Interesting features along the walk have been created by the dolerite extrusion of the Great Whin Sill which extends across much of northern England. The scent of juniper berries near High Force on a summer's day can be almost overpowering.

From Bowlees Visitor Centre go down to the river and cross Wynch Bridge. Turn right, upstream past Low Force. Continue along the riverbank to High Force then retrace your steps back to Holwick Head Bridge. Cross the bridge, climb up to the B6277 and turn right for about a quarter of a mile then left on a side road to Dirt Pit. Turn right and follow a farm track back to the visitor centre.

Low Force.

Swaledale (p.92)

Kisdon Hill
4¹/₂ miles – moderate – 2¹/₂ hours

This walk follows part of the Swaledale 'corpse road' from Keld and returns along the Pennine Way around the graceful contours of Kisdon Hill.

From Keld follow the B6270 downhill to a footpath sign on the left marked 'Muker'. Take the rough track, across a stream then bear right towards the hillside. Continue along an elevated track until you reach a signpost indicating the Pennine Way and turn left. Follow a level path across the limestone outcrop (caution: slippery when wet). Look across the valley on the right. Ruined Crackpot Hall is opposite and later Kisdon Force can be reached by a short detour. Go through natural woodland, then uphill along a narrow lane into Keld.

Thwaite and Muker
3 miles – easy – 1^1/$_2$ hours

This walk could be linked to the one previous by joining it at the Pennine Way sign near Kisdon Farm above Thwaite, to make a figure-of-eight route. It visits two of the most attractive and unspoilt villages in Swaledale.

Follow Pennine Way signs north-east through a complex of fields from Thwaite, then climb above Doctor Wood. Keep left of Kisdon Farm then right at the signpost (left if linking to the Kisdon Hill walk, returning to this point later). Go down a farm track into Muker (pub nearby). Do not go as far as the main road, but turn right along a narrow back street to reach open fields. Use stiles and walk in single file along the grassy path. On reaching the road turn right as far as the bridge, but do not cross. Keep ahead on a field path into Thwaite.

Marrick Priory
5^1/$_2$ miles – Moderate/easy – 2^3/$_4$ hours

Thwaite.

Here is a walk which can be linked with a visit to Reeth. It quickly leaves the crowds behind, calling at a tranquil priory along the way.

Walk down to Reeth Bridge and turn left on to a field path. Climb up to High Fremington Farm and keep to the rear of the farm buildings. Follow a path across a series of fields as far as a narrow lane and turn left, uphill (watch out for traffic). At a sharp left hand bend at the top of the hill, go right at a footpath sign and cross three fields. Follow the path as far as a stone stile giving access into a lane and turn right for Marrick. Take the first right into the village, then right again following a sign to 'Marrick Priory'. Cross a field then go down a flight of stone steps at the side of a wood. Walk past farm buildings and the priory to their access road. Turn left on to the road, go through an iron gate and immediately right into a field. There is no path, but the right-of-way can be followed diagonally left by lining up stiles and gates across a series of fields. Go down to the road and turn left for about 70yd then right over a stile. Follow the riverbank, upstream to the road bridge. Cross the road and go through a stile, bear right on a footpath to Reeth.

Wensleydale (p.110)

Cam Road and the Pennine Way
6 miles – moderate – 3 hours

The walk is from the National Park Information Centre in Hawes. Turn right into the main street and walk as far as the public toilets. Turn left through a small car park and cross two fields in the direction of the Wensleydale Creameries. Cross the road by the creamery to follow a narrow path across a series of small fields, using stiles to keep on course. On reaching the main road, turn left for about 150yd then left again, uphill on a broad unpaved track; this is Cam Road. Follow the track for a couple of miles, pausing only to admire the all-round views. Pass the upper limits of a pine plantation and at Ten End look out for a cairn on your left, marked faintly with the letters P/W; this is the Pennine Way. Turn sharp left along the grassy path over gently rising ground, then downhill with good views of Upper Wensleydale. On reaching a farm lane, turn right as far as a road, then right again for about 100yd. Climb over a stile on your left and follow a profusion of Pennine Way signs through Gayle village. Keep to the left of Hawes Church and enter the village beneath an archway. The car park and information centre are along the street on the right.

Semer Water
4 miles – easy – 2 hours

Start from Bainbridge and follow the cul-de-sac road south from the village green, past Dame's School Cottage, then along a private drive marked with a footpath sign. Bear right from the house, out into open fields. Follow signs to the right of a large house and across more fields, aiming for an old barn. Go through a stile on its right; turn left along the road past Semerdale Hall and through Countersett. In Countersett, turn left, downhill to Semer Water. Cross the triple-arched road bridge, then left through a narrow stile and follow a signposted path along the riverbank. Cross a ladder stile and climb to the right, away from the river by following waymarked posts. At the side road, turn left as far as the main road and left again into Bainbridge.

Semer Water by monnlight.

Aysgarth and West Burton
5 miles – easy – 2 or 3 hours

This walk visits unspoilt West Burton and enjoys quiet views of Aysgarth's Middle and Lower Falls from the less frequented south bank of the Ure. From the car park cross the river and climb the steps to Aysgarth Church, then go towards and across the main road. Using stiles cross a series of fields until you reach Eshington

Bridge. Cross the bridge and turn right on a path signposted to West Burton. On reaching the village, bear left then right as far as the wide village green. Follow a lane from the lower end of the green down to the waterfall. Cross a narrow stone bridge, then left and right on a path past Barrack Wood. Left along a farm lane and right on a footpath signposted 'Edgley': way-marked stiles and gates indicate the route. Turn right at the road for about 130yd, then diagonally left across a field as far as the main road. Left over Hestholme Bridge and right on a waymarked path on its far side. Follow the riverbank above the falls back to Aysgarth.

Nidderdale (p.134)

Lofthouse and Gouthwaite Reservoir
5 miles - Easy - 2¹/₂ hours

From Lofthouse follow the road across both the Nidd and How Stean Beck, then turn left and left again along farm lanes on the west side of the dale as far as Ramsgill. Left in the village to Bouthwaite and its views along the reservoir, then left again to follow a series of paths and then the valley road back to Lofthouse.

Pateley Bridge and the Panorama Walk
3¹/₂ miles – easy/moderate – 2 hours

This signposted walk climbs past the village cemetery towards the ruin of the first church built in Pateley Bridge, then swings left along the Panorama Walk to join a minor road leading left to Wath. Go down to the river and turn left along its left bank as far as Pateley Bridge.

Foster Beck Mill Inn, Pateley Bridge.

Brimham Rocks
1 to 3 miles – easy – 1¹/₂ hours

A complex of footpaths between the B6265 Ripon Road, and Summer Bridge on the B6165 can, with the aid of the OS map, be used to enjoy a number of walks, all leading to the strange formations of Brimham Rocks (Café and information centre). Limited wheelchair access.

Wharfedale (p.141)

Buckden and Upper Wharfedale
5 miles – moderate – 2¹/₂ - 3 hours

Park in the official car park above Buckden's village green and take an upward slanting track, signposted 'To Buckden Pike and Cray'. Pausing only to admire the views of Upper Wharfedale, climb out on to a grassy terrace. Ignore any paths to the right and walk on until you see a steep path to the left, down to Cray. Follow this over a stream and cross the road, then go behind the White Lion Inn to find a level path beyond the last building. Follow this path, above a limestone crag cut only by narrow gullies, as far as a turning left to Scar House. Go through the farmyard and down its access track into the dale bottom. At Hubberholme, call at the church then cross the bridge to turn left past the George Inn. Follow the road for about ¹/₂ mile then turn left through a gate on to a fieldpath signposted to Buckden Bridge. Turn left over the bridge into Buckden.

Conistone's Pastures
5 miles – easy/moderate – 3 hours

From the centre of Conistone, walk along the Grassington road for about 100yd, past the Methodist chapel and turn left at the side of a cottage. Follow a cart track signposted 'Grassington', uphill and then ahead on a grassy path, following the direction of fingerposts. Go over a stone stile then around the upper limits of a rocky gorge. Climb a ladder stile then gradually bear right across the rocky pathless upland pastures.

Keep well to the left of the woodland boundary as far as a boundary wall in sight of Grassington and at right-angles to your route. Do not cross this wall, but turn sharp left, away from it on to a grassy path across a series of upland pastures; cross field boundaries by their stiles or gates. Cross a stile and go left as indicated by a signpost, towards Conistone. Go down into a narrow dry valley and follow it all the way to Conistone.

Bolton Abbey and Strid Wood
6¹/₂ miles - easy - 4 hours

From Bolton Abbey village follow the road as far as the Cavendish Memorial and turn right then left, down a flight of steps towards the riverside meadows. Walk upstream to the Cavendish Pavilion, pay the small entry fee, pick up a nature trail leaflet and, following green markers, walk into the woods.

Walk on through the woods, changing to purple then yellow waymarks to follow the path past The Strid and out over a footbridge into an open field. Turn right across the stone bridge disguising a water pipe and on the far side turn right again. Walk downstream through a wood of predominantly beech and oak trees. Cross a wooden stile then right along the road for about 130yd, over a road bridge then right along a grassy path signposted to Cavendish and Bolton Abbey.

Continue downstream beyond a wooden bridge (cross only if calling at the Pavilion for refreshments). Climb up to the road again. Follow it, over a ford, then right as signposted to Bolton Priory. Cross the river, either by the footbridge or the Friar's Stepping Stones if the river is low enough and walk up to the abbey ruins. Follow the path to the left and away from the abbey to a hole in the high boundary wall. Go through it and turn left, back along the road to the village. Limited wheelchair access.

Bolton Priory.

176

Airedale (p.154)

Malham Cove and Gordale Scar
5 miles – moderate/strenuous – 3 hours

From the centre of Malham, cross the hump-backed road bridge, then left along the lane past the Youth Hostel. Follow a waymarked path through fields, then left down to the stream and over a clapper bridge. Turn right along a path to Malham Cove and left up a stepped path. Climb a stone stile and turn right across the limestone pavement. (Warning: Take extra care on the broken surface of the pavement, especially along the edge of the cove, and in wet or windy weather.) At the far end, climb a ladder stile and bear right uphill on a waymarked grassy path. Cross ladder stiles on both sides of the road and follow another grassy path downhill as far as Gordale Bridge. Cross the bridge, go left through a gate to follow a path up to Gordale Scar; return to the bridge. Go through a gate on the left at the far side of the bridge, down to Janet's Foss. Follow the waymarked woodland and field path back to Malham.

Cracoe Fell 6 miles
strenuous – 3 hours

(Do not attempt this walk during grouse shooting, or at times of high fire risk. From Skipton end of Cracoe village, turn left, and left again along a narrow winding lane. Right at the T-junction along a track towards the open fell. Go through a gate and bear left away from a sheep pen. Zig-zag uphill on the trackless moor, aiming towards the prominent skyline pinnacle.

Climb a ladder stile behind the pinnacle and turn right, by the side of a gently descending moorland boundary wall. Go through a gap in the wall and descend to the right on a recessed track marked with blue topped stakes. Turn right at a track junction, then over a stile to follow a fieldpath signposted to Cracoe. Right through a narrow gate opposite Rylstone Church. Follow the path across one field, through another gate and along a leafy lane to Cracoe.

The Leeds-Liverpool Canal and the Pennine Way from Gargrave
7½ miles – 3-3½ hours - easy

Walk along the Malham road from the centre of Gargrave and turn left along the canal towpath. Climb up to the main road, turn right along it, then left along a side road. Go through a wooden stile on the left and right along the towpath. Cross the canal at Bridge 165, to walk along the opposite bank, following its contour-hugging course through fields. Go under the A59, turn right across the next bridge (number 160) and walk past East Marton Church. Cross the A59 in front of Cross Keys Inn. Follow the lane down to and over the canal following 'Pennine Way' signs; bear right away from the canal. Still following 'Pennine Way' signs for a little over 1½ miles, cross a series of grassy fields. Join a farm lane; follow it to the right, then over a railway bridge. On the far side cross a stile on the right and walk diagonally across the fields to Gargrave school. Turn left along the access lane, past the church, over the River Aire where the main part of Gargrave is to the right.

Skipton Marina.

Malham
(8 miles, 4 hours)

It starts by the bridge and follows the river downstream for a little way to a gate where a signposted path leads left into Gordale, alongside the stream and through Wedber Wood. Janet's Foss lies at the head of the wood which is set out as a nature trail with plaques explaining the natural features. Above Janet's Foss the path climbs up to and crosses the road before entering the meadow below Gordale Scar. As mentioned earlier the best way up the waterfall is to climb the buttress on the left (when facing); above it a scree slope leads to a field dotted with limestone outcrops and boulders. Pass through this field on a path of springy turf to the road. Turn right along the road and walk to Malham Tarn, but afterwards steps must be retraced until a path is seen diverging on the right. Follow this back to the road where a right-hand turn and then left beyond a gate leads down past Water Sinks (where the river disappears underground), and into a dry valley leading to the top of Malham Cove. The way down is to walk (with care) to the right, across the limestone pavement to its far end and after crossing a stile on the left follow zig-zags down into Malhamdale and back to the village.

Scenic Car drives

Ribblesdale (p.20)

The Lower Ribble and Hodder Valleys
50 miles

This pleasant drive is mostly along quiet by-ways and country roads, visiting pretty villages where time stands still, in marked contrast to the bustle of nearby industrial Lancashire.

Starting in Whalley at the junction of the A59 and A671 (abbey, restaurants and shops), take the B6246 to Great Mitton and turn left on the B6243 to Longridge. Turn right in the village and climb by a minor road across its fell (scenic view points, picnic places, pub and hang-gliding viewing). Go downhill and turn left at the next cross-roads to drive through Bashall Eaves (Browsholme Hall is on the right) then on to Whitewell (inn). Turn right for Dunsop Bridge (trout farm), where a diversion can be made to the Trough of Bowland and its fells. From Dunsop Bridge take the valley road east of Newton (pub) and join the B6478. Take this road to Slaidburn (interesting church, pub and riverside picnic area); continue across Stephen Moor to a road junction short of Wigglesworth (pub). Turn right for Bolton-by-Bowland (interesting church, cafés)

and on to Sawley (ruined abbey, riverside restaurant). Do not join the main A59, but bear right in Sawley for Grindleton and Waddington (pubs, cafés, riverside strolling). At Waddington turn left for Clitheroe (shops, market, castle, etc), then join the A59 for the return to Whalley.

Cattle near Ribblehead.

Lune Valley (p.40)

The Lune Valley and its Side Dales
84 miles

From Ingleton take the A65 as far as Kirkby Lonsdale (cafés, shops), then right along the A683 to Sedbergh (pubs, cafés, information centre, market - Wednesday). Follow a narrow unclassified road north-westwards into the Lune Gorge; cross the river by the ancient Crook of Lune Bridge, then right on the A685 through Tebay to Ravenstonedale (inn).

Follow a short unclassified road to the right through the dale up to the A683 and turn right again. Follow this road, completing the circuit of the Howgill Fells, into Sedbergh. Left along Dentdale by an unclassified road, Dent village is on the south side of the dale (shops, cafés, pubs, walks). Climb out beyond the dale, head to join the B6255, turn right continuing ahead at the T-junction near Ribblehead (inn and good views of the viaduct, also the Hill Inn at Chapel-le-Dale). Downhill with good views of Ingleborough on your left, past White Scar Cave (show cave with limited access to wheelchairs), back to Ingleton (shops, cafés, pubs, nature trail).

178

Teesdale (p.58)

Through the Northern Dales
84 miles

The drive starts and finishes in historic Barnard Castle. Follow the A67 to Bowes (Castle and Roman remains), then via the A66 across wild Stainmore to Brough (interesting market town, cafés, shops, pubs) and on to Appleby (shops, cafés, pubs, castle and Rare Breeds Conservation Centre).

Using side roads, go through Dufton and Skirwith to Melmerby and turn right along the A686 across Hartside Pass (café).

In Alston (cafés, pubs, interesting market cross, narrow gauge railway), follow the A689 through Nenthead (lead mining trail) into Weardale, calling at the Killhope Wheel Lead Mining Centre along the way. Turn right at St. John's Chapel and climb across Langdon Common into Teesdale. Divert to Cow Green Reservoir (viewpoint, nature trail), then follow the B6277, calling at High Force (waterfall, inn) and Bowlees (visitor centre, Low Force, pub).

On through Middleton-in-Teesdale (interesting ex-lead mining village, cafés, shops, pubs). Continue down the valley by way of Eggleston (interesting old village) to Barnard Castle (castle, Bowes Museum, shops, cafés, restaurants, hotels).

Market stand, Barnard Castle.

Swaledale (p.92)

Through Swaledale
42 miles

At a first glance it might not seem possible to follow a circuit around Swaledale without using the same road continuously, but with the exception of a short stretch of the B6270 near Reeth and by using unclassified side roads, the dale's varied beauties can be explored without seeing the same place twice.

The drive starts in Richmond; take the minor road north-west from the town centre, out on to Richmond Moor above Whitcliffe Scar (view point accessible only by footpath) and go steeply down into Marske. Continue via Fremington into Reeth (folk museum, village green, cafés, pubs) and turn right for Arkengarthdale. Drive along the dale, through Langthwaite (pubs) and across the moors to the Tan Hill Inn (view point). Left at the T-junction and down West Stones Dale to the B6270; turn left along the dale road, through Keld. Thwaite (restaurant), Muker (pub) and Gunnerside (pubs, cafés, art gallery, shop and Gunnerside Beck walking trail). Continue to follow the valley bottom road, through Feetham, Healaugh and Reeth. Bear right to cross the river and still following the B6270, left through Grinton (pub) and then joining the A6108 along an increasingly wooded stretch of the Swale back to Richmond (castle, shops, cafés, pubs, museum).

Langthwaite, Arkengarthdale.

Wensleydale (p.110)

Around Wensleydale
93 miles

From Ripon follow the B6265 for 3 miles, maybe detouring left to visit Studley Park and Fountains Abbey. Right from the B6265 on to unclassified roads through Kirkby Malzeard and Grewelthorpe to Masham (pubs and cafés). Left on the A6108 through Middleham (ancient castle, pubs, cafés, shops) and over the suspension bridge to Leyburn (pubs, cafés, shops). Left along the

A684, through West Witton (Knights Templar's Chapel) and Aysgarth (scenic waterfalls, museum, cafés, car park and National Park Information Centre); through Bainbridge (possible diversion left to Semer Water) and Hawes (car parking, National Park Information Centre, museum, ropeworks, market, shops, pubs, restaurants, cafés). Right by minor road to Hardraw (pub, scenic waterfall), then along the north side of the dale through Sedbusk to Askrigg (James Herriot connections, pubs, cafés). Through Carperby (Wheatsheaf Hotel) to Castle Bolton (historic castle, restaurant) and via Redmire to Leyburn. Left along the A684 as far as Bedale (pubs, shops etc). Right for the B6268 (possible diversion to Thorpe Perrow Arboretum). Right again at the junction with the B6267 and left along the A6108 back to Ripon.

King's Arms, Askrigg.

Wharfedale (p.141)

Through Wharfedale
100 miles

As there is only one road through Wharfedale, the B6160, this drive has been designed to also cover the Washburn Valley, part of Nidderdale and in order to create a circular tour, the route enters Upper Wharfedale by way of Wensleydale and remote Bishopdale. The drive starts and finishes at Ilkley. Drive down the A65 to Otley and turn left along the B6451, through the Washburn Valley, over the A59 and on to Summer Bridge, where a diversion can be made to Brimham Rocks (National Trust). Left along the B6165 to Pateley Bridge (Panorama Walk, cafés etc). Right on the B6265, then by unclassified roads north through Kirkby

Malzeard to Masham (pubs, cafés). Left along the A6108, past Jervaulx Abbey and through Middleham (castle, cafés, pubs, shops) to Leyburn.

Left by the A684 along Wensleydale to Aysgarth (waterfalls, museum, cafés, pub). Minor road south to West Burton in Bishopdale (interesting unspoilt village); right on the B6160 through Cray (Warning: Steep descent by narrow road) into Buckden (pub). Valley road through Kettlewell (pubs, cafés), past Kilnsey (pub, waterpark), to Threshfield (interesting village) and maybe divert to Grassington (interesting village, pubs, cafés, shops). Continue by the B6160 to Bolton Abbey (interesting ruins, restaurant, café etc). Cross the A59 and turn left on the A65 in Addingham, Ilkley is about 2 miles further down the road (shops, hotels, pubs, restaurants, museum, walks on Ilkley Moor).

Airedale (p.154)

Around Airedale
58 miles

As a number of narrow, winding single track roads are used on this drive, great care and attention should be given to road conditions at all times and consideration given to other road users.

From Skipton follow the A65 to Gargrave, and take the valley road north to Malham (car park, pubs, cafés, Malham Cove, Gordale Scar, Janet's Foss, short walks, information centre), and turn right over the hump-backed bridge. Left beyond the Youth Hostel, steeply uphill and left to Malham Tarn (small car park, view point, wildfowl, short walks).

Ahead and across Malham Moor, then steeply downhill to Settle (pubs, cafés, shops, museum, walks). A65 to Gargrave (pubs, shops, cafés, riverside strolls), and south by unclassified road to Broughton. Right for a quarter of a mile along the A59, then left by minor roads through Elslack and across Carleton Moor to Lothersdale (pub, interesting mill). Minor road into Crosshills, left on the A629 to Kildwick (restaurant, interesting church), to Skipton (pubs, shops, cafés, restaurants, castle, museum, interesting church, markets).

Useful information for visitors

Abbeys, Castles, and other Historic Buildings

Appleby Castle
Appleby, on the A66 Penrith-Brough road
Tel: (017683) 51402
Norman keep set in attractive gardens. Examples of Roman armour and medieval furniture. Rare Breeds Survival Trust Centre.
Open: Easter Friday to Easter Monday, 10am-5pm. Special party rates by arrangement. Free car park. Picnic areas.

Barden Tower
Barden, Wharfedale, on B6160 2¾ miles N.W. of Bolton Abbey.
Tel: (01756) 710533
11th-century hunting lodge above the River Wharfe. Part of the building is still inhabited and offers accommodation and refreshments.
Open: Artist's studio, daily May to October, by appointment other times. Drawing, painting and etching courses held at certain times.

Barnard Castle
(English Heritage)
Barnard Castle, on the A67 in the centre of the town. A Norman stronghold on the north bank of the River Tees.
Open: mid-March to mid-October, (weekdays) 9.30am-6.30pm, (Sunday) 2-6.30pm; October to March, (weekdays) 9.30am-4pm. (Sunday) 2-4pm; also Sunday, April to Sept. 9.30am-6.30pm. Charge for admission.

Blanchland Abbey
Blanchland on the B6306, 8 miles south of Hexham.

Remains of a fortified 12th-century abbey incorporated into various buildings within the village. The Lord Crewe Arms was once the abbey guest house.

Bolton Abbey
Wharfedale 6½ miles E. of Skipton, approached via A59.
Tel: (01756) 710533
Attractive riverside ruins of Augustinian priory.
Open to the public at all times.

Bolton Castle
Castle Bolton, Wensleydale. 4½ miles N.E. of Aysgarth on Reeth road.
Tel: (01969) 623332
14th-century castle which was besieged by the parliamentary troops in the Civil War. Public rooms now used as a restaurant.
Open: March to mid-Nov., daily 10am-5pm.

Bowes Castle
(English Heritage)
Bowes on the A66, 4 miles S.W. of Barnard Castle. Massive 12th-century stone keep built on site of Roman fort of Lavatræ to command the eastern access to Stainmore.
Open: daylight hours. Free admission.

Brough Castle
(English Heritage)
Brough, 16 miles N.E. of M6 junction 38 at junction of A685 and A66.
Tel: (0191) 2611585
Norman keep built on the site of a Roman fort.

Clitheroe Castle
Clitheroe, Lancashire. Ruins of medieval castle in public gardens.
Free Access during daylight hours.

East Riddlesden Hall
(National Trust)
On A650, 1 mile S.E. of Keighley.
Tel: (01535) 607075
17th-century manor house and banqueting hall. Great barn.
Open: April to October, Wed. to Sunday; Bank Holiday Monday (closed Good Friday) 2-6; June, July, August 11am-6pm. Educational visits; Thursdays and Fridays all season by appointment.

Eggleston Abbey
(English Heritage)
Approached by Rokeby Park road 1 mile S. of Barnard Castle. Picturesque ruin set on a hill above the south bank of the River Tees. The greater part of the 13th to 14th-century nave survives.
Open: mid-March to mid-October, weekdays 9.30am-6.30pm, Sun. 2-6.30pm; Oct. to March, weekdays 9.30am-4pm, Sun. 2-4pm. Free admission, Guide book available.

Fountains Abbey and Studley Royal
(National Trust) 3 miles S.W. of Ripon off B6265 to Pateley Bridge. The largest monastic ruin in Britain with landscaped gardens. World Heritage site.
Open: Oct. to March, daily (except Christmas Eve and Christmas Day) 10am-4pm; April to June and September, daily 10am-7pm; July and August, daily 10am-8pm.

Jervaulx Abbey
On A6108 between Leyburn and Masham. 12th-century Cistercian abbey, almost completely obliterated by Henry VIII, but the ground plan and a number of carved

stones still remain. Beautiful setting on the banks of the River Ure.
Tel: (01677) 460391

Knaresborough Castle
Castle Yard, Knaresborough.
Tel: (01423) 503340
Home of Plantagenet kings, later ransacked by Cromwell during the Civil War. *Open: Easter weekend,. Spring Bank Holiday, then from late spring holiday to 30 Sept.*

Marrick Priory
Swaledale, ½ mile S.W. of Marrick village. Reached by stone causeway from Marrick village. Tranquil situation on the River Swale. *Exterior only, not open to the public.*

Middleham Castle
(English Heritage)
Situated in Middleham on A6108 Leyburn to Ripon road. Impressive ruin of 12th-century castle, which once was the home of King Richard III.
Tel: (01969) 623899
Open: mid-March to mid-Oct., weekdays 9.30am-6.30pm, Sunday 2-6.30pm; Oct. to March, weekdays 9.30am-4pm, Sun. 2-4pm.

Richmond Castle
(English Heritage)
Richmond, North Yorkshire. Massive Norman keep founded by Alan Rufus.
Tel: (01748) 822493
Open: mid-March to mid-Oct., weekdays 9.30am-6.30pm, Sunday 2-6pm; Oct. to March, weekdays 9.30am-4pm, Sunday 2-4pm.

Ripley Castle
3½ miles N. of Harrogate on A61.
Tel: (01423) 770152
Home of the Ingilby family. The nearby

village has a strong French atmosphere. *Open: gardens, April to mid-Oct., daily 11am-5.30pm.* **Castle**: *April to May, Sat. and Sunday 11.30am-4.30pm; June to mid-Oct., daily (except Monday and Friday) 11.30am-4.30pm; Bank Holidays in season 11am-4.30pm.*

Rokeby Park
Off A66 about 3 miles S.E. of Barnard Castle. Palladian house built in 1736. Paintings and unique collection of needlework. The ruins of Mortham Tower are within the grounds. *Open throughout the summer.*

Sawley Abbey
(English Heritage) Sawley, on the A59, 3 miles N.E of Clitheroe. Ruins of medieval monastery. *Free access during daylight hours.*

Skipton Castle
Centre of Skipton town. 11th-century castle, restored between 1650-1675 by Lady Anne Clifford. Maintained by local organisation. Tel: (01756) 792442 *Open: all year (except Christmas Day and Good Friday), weekdays, 10am-dusk, Sunday 2-6pm (or dusk if earlier).*

Whalley Abbey
Whalley, off A59 4 miles S. of Clitheroe. Manor house used as a retreat centre. Attractive flower gardens, gift shop and craft centre. *Open: Easter to Oct., weekdays 11.30am-4.30pm Sunday 1-4.30pm.*

Accommodation

Wherever you choose accommodation in the Yorkshire Dales you will find a warm welcome and a hospitality which is known throughout the world. A comprehensive Accommodation Guide is published by the Yorkshire Dales National Park Authority in conjunction with the Yorkshire Dales Tourist Association. Simple and group accommodation is available at Youth Hostels and Bunk House Barns throughout the dales. For details, contact:

Youth Hostels Association
Trevelyan House, St Albans, Herts AL1 2DY Tel: (01727) 55215

Some **Tourist Information Centres**, such as Settle, operate a 'Book-a-Bed' service. For a small fee they will find you the right sort of accommodation. Information on accommodation outside the Yorkshire Dales Nat. Park is obtainable from tourist boards as listed:

Northumbria Tourist Board,
9 Osborne Terrace, Jesmond, Newcastle upon Tyne, NE2 1NT Tel: (01632) 817744

North-West Tourist Board,
The Last Drop Village, Bromley Cross, Bolton, Lancashire BL7 9PZ Tel: (01204) 591511

Yorkshire and Humberside Tourist Board
312 Tadcaster Road, York YO2 2HF Tel: (01904) 707961

Archaeological Sites

Bremetennacum
Ribchester on B6245, 4 miles N. of Blackburn. Roman fort with only the perimeter wall visible and partially excavated granary. *Open: during daylight hours.*

Hanging Walls of Mark Anthony
Kirkland, 9 miles N.W of Appleby, (NY652322). Fine examples of prehistoric cultivation terraces.

Ilkley Moor
Ilkley Moor has innumerable prehistoric remains, and a glance at a map will indicate these.

Long Meg and Her Daughters
Little Salkeld, 4½ miles N.E. of Penrith Oval stone circle with 27 of a probable 60 stones still standing. Long Meg is the tallest stone, 10ft high, with symbolic cup-and-ring carvings. (NY571372)

Swastika Stone
(SE095470) An enigmatic carving on a prominent rock.

Twelve Apostles
(SE126451) Stone circle approached by path from White Wells to Baildon.

White Wells
(SE109468) Bath house erected by 18th-century philanthropist for inhabitants of Ilkley.

Virosidum
Bainbridge, Wensleydale, (SD937902) Roman fortification visible on prominent mound east of Bainbridge village.

Whitley Castle
B6292, 2 miles N. of Alston (NY695487) Excellent example of a well fortified Roman fort.

Balloon Flights

Airborne Adventures Ltd
43 Westwood, Carleton, Skipton, North Yorkshire, BD23 3DW Tel: (01756) 701566

Black Sheep Balloons
Tel: (01756) 748106

Bird Watching

Courses in bird watching are organised by:

Bird Guide
Ashville, Rose Bank, Burley-in-Wharfedale, West Yorkshire

Field Studies Council
The Malham Tarn Field Centre, Settle, North Yorkshire, BD24 9PU

YHA
Trevelyan House, 8 St Stephen's Hill, St Albans, Herts

Boating and sailing

Calder Valley Cruising
Barge Branwell The Marina, Hebden Bridge Tel: (01422) 845557 Horse drawn traditional canal barge. Lunch and tea cruises a speciality. *From Easter to Christmas.*

Derwent Reservoir
Derwentdale Club and day sailing. Picnic areas.

Foulridge Canal Cruises
Canal Wharf, Foulridge, Colne, Lancs BB8 7PP Tel: (01282) 844033 The 'Marton Emperor' offers a one and a half hour cruise along the Leeds-Liverpool Canal. *Sun. and Thurs. throughout most of the year.*

Knaresborough
Rowing boats available for hire throughout the summer months on the River Nidd.

Leeds and Liverpool Canal
Pleasure boats available for holiday hire from:

Black Prince
Narrowboats Ltd., Silsden, Steeton

British Waterways Bank
Newton Lock Gargrave.
Tel: (01756) 790829

Pennine Boat Trips of Skipton
Tel/fax: (01756) 790829

Pennine Cruisers
Coach Street
Skipton.
Tel: (01756) 795478

Snaygill Boats
Skipton Road
Bradford, Skipton.
Tel: (01756) 795150

Yorkshire Dales Hire Cruises
Bank Newton, Gargrave
Skipton BD23 3NT

Semer Water
Countersett, Raydale, 1 mile south of Bainbridge, via A684. Popular picnic area with unofficial small craft use.

Buildings and Gardens

Opening times are subject to alterations so check locally for further details.

Browsholme Hall
Bashall Eaves, Near Clitheroe. Home of the Parker family since 1507. Tours conducted by members of the family. *Open: Easter, Spring Bank Holiday and 1 week either side of Summer Bank Holiday. Parties of at least four by* appointment from mid-May to end of Sept.

Constable Burton Hall and Gardens
3½ miles east of Leyburn on A684. Georgian hall. *Gardens open to the public, but the hall by appointment only.*

East Riddlesden Hall
A650, 1 mile N.E. of Keighley. 17th-century manor house. Tithe barn, fishpond, grounds. Art gallery. National Trust.

Harlow Car Gardens
Harrogate, on S.W. edge of town approached from B6162. Run by the Northern Horticultural Society. The gardens specialise in testing new varieties of fruits and vegetables as well as flowers and shrubs. Free coach and car parks.

Markenfield Hall
Off the A61, 1½ miles south-west of Ripon. Moated manor and farmhouse. One time home of the Marken-fields who lost everything for supporting the abortive 'Rising of the North' in 1569.

Newby Hall
Newby, 4 miles south of Ripon on the Borough-bridge old road. Magnificent hall with landscaped gardens. Built in 1690s, enlarged and redecorated in 1760s by Robert Adam. *Open: to the public during summer months. Gardens and restaurant, Easter and April to Oct. 11am-5.30pm, every day except Monday, but open Bank Holiday Mondays.* Hall and train: *April to October every day except Monday; also Easter and Bank Holiday Mondays, 1-5pm. Plant stall, steamboat,* children's playground, steam railway (miniature).

Norton Conyers
Near Wath, 3½ miles north of Ripon off A61 Fine Jacobean house and garden. *Open: all year, Monday to Friday; April to Oct., Sat. and Sun. 2-5.30pm. Garden centre and refreshments.*

Parcevall Hall Gardens
Skyreholme, near Appletreewick, 10 miles north of Ilkley. Secluded gardens in Trollers Ghyll.
Tel: (01756) 720311
Open: Easter to October, daily 10am-6pm.

Stonyhurst College
Hurst Green, 4 miles from Clitheroe.
Tel: Stonyhurst 345
Catholic public school founded in 1593, but main building dates from 1594. *Open: to visitors by prior appointment.*

Thorp Perrow
Arboretum, Bedale, North Yorkshire. One of the finest collections of trees in Britain.

Country Parks and Visitor Centres

Beacon Fell Country Park
8 miles north of Preston and signposted from Longridge, (SD568429) Conifer woods, forest walks, viewpoint, picnic areas, refreshments. *Open all year.*

Bowlees Visitor Centre
Bowlees, Upper Teesdale, on B6277, 3 miles N.W. of Middleton-in-Teesdale. Visual display of natural history of Upper Teesdale. Attractively laid out museum in converted chapel. Picnic site nearby. *Open: summer months only.*

Cove Centre
Malham.
Tel: (01729) 830363
Craft workshops, Café.
Open throughout the year.

The Dales Centre
Grassington, near Skipton.
Tel: (01756) 752312
Holiday accommodation. Caving and climbing instruction. Slide shows and other events in the evenings.

Hazel Brow Farm
Low Row, Richmond, North Yorkshire
DL11 6NE
Tel: (01748) 886412 or 886224. Working dales farm, nature hunt and riverside walk.

How Stean Gorge
10 miles N.W of Pateley Bridge, Nidderdale. Narrow gorge near the head of Nidderdale, skilfully laid out with walks and footbridges. Children's play area. Car Park. *Open: all the year.*

Kilnsey Water Park
Kilnsey, near Skipton
Tel: (01756) 752150
Trout hatchery, picnic site, freshwater aquarium, fishing. *Open all year, daily 9.30am-5pm.*

Lightwater Valley Country Theme Park
3 miles north of Ripon on the A6108.
Tel: 24 hour Hot line (01765) 635368. Adventure theme park, farm, restaurants and shops. Admission price includes all rides. *Open: April and May, Easter week, weekends and Bank Holidays; June, July and Aug., daily; Sept., week-ends 10.30am-3.30pm.*

Penistone Hill Country Park
Haworth, ½ mile south-west of village. Open moorland on edge of village.

Rare Breeds Survival Trust Centre
Appleby Castle, Appleby, on A66 Penrith to Brough road. Tel: (017683) 51402 Collection of rare breeds of domestic farm animals, wildfowl, pheasants, poultry and owls. Beautifully laid out grounds. Free car park. Picnic areas and tea rooms. *Open: Easter Friday to Easter Monday 10.30am-5pm; May to end Sept., daily 10.30am-5pm. Special party rates by arrangement.*

Slurring Rocks Country Park
Hardcastle Crags, Hebden Bridge. (SD988291) Attractive wooded valley and gritstone gorge. Refreshments nearby.

Otter Trust
Vale House Farm, near Bowes, County Durham Tel: (01833) 628339 Otter rehabilitation centre set in 230 acres of upland farm land along the River Greta. Breeding grounds of moorland birds. Rare breeds including Highland cattle, Exmoor ponies and White-faced Woodland sheep. Dogs not allowed. *Open: daily late May to end October, 10.30am-6.00pm. otter feeding times; 12 noon and 3.30pm.*

Wensleydale Creamery Visitor Centre
Gayle Lane, Hawes, North Yorkshire DL8 3RN Tel: (01969) 667664 Demonstrations of Wensleydale cheese making. Shop, restaurant and 'cheese tastings'. Accessible to the disabled. *Open all year: Mon-Sat 9.30am to 5pm; Sunday 10am to 4.30pm.*

Whorlton Lido
4 miles south-east of Barnard Castle. On privately owned picnic site. Has narrow gauge railway on south bank of River Tees.

Wycoller Visitor Centre
Off Haworth Road, 3 miles from Colne. Sensitive preservation of an unspoilt hamlet.

Yorkshire Flight Centre
Knaresborough. Tel: (01423) 340664 Flight-deck simulator.

Cycle Hire
Cycle hire is usually available at daily or weekly rates. For more information *Cycling in the Yorkshire Dales* (R. Harris, MPC) gives a mile by mile account of routes and tour planning with a comprehensive list of cycle hirers.

Grassington
Mountain Bike Hire, 5 Chapel St. Tel: (01756)752592

Hawes
Dales Cycle Hire, Tel: (019697) 487

Ingleton
Richard's Cycles, The Square. Tel: (01468) 41094

Settle
Settle Cycles, Duke Street. Tel: (017292) 2216

Wharfedale
The Dales Centre Tennant Arms, Kilnsey. Tel: (01756) 752301 or 752312

Dales Rail and Bus Services
A fully integrated rail and bus service operates on certain dates throughout the summer based on the Leeds to Carlisle line with connections from Preston and Blackburn to Hellifield. Intermediate stations of Settle to Carlisle line are open for Dales Rail. Information is also available from the Yorkshire and Humberside Tourist Board, Northumbrian Tourist Board and North-West Tourist Boards (see under Accommodation for addresses and telephone numbers. There are organised walks planned each year, timed to start and finish with convenient trains and buses. By careful use of the Dales Rail Time Table more ambitious routes may be planned. Further details can be obtained from Yorkshire Dales National Park Committee Information Centres, or:

Railway

Skipton Tel: (01756) 792809

D. Whaites 12 High Hill Grove, Settle

Dales Rail Yorkshire Dales National Park, Colvend, Hebden Road, Grassington BD23 5LB Tel: (01756) 752748

Friends of Dales Rail c/o 3 Rochester Terrace Leeds LS6 3DF

Fishing
Most rivers with game fish are privately owned but fishing permits can be bought locally. Rod licences are issued by the various water authorities (addresses below), who also allow game and coarse fishing on reservoirs and stretches of river under their control. Each authority publishes a descriptive leaflet. Owners of other lakes and millpools, such as Malham Tarn and Foster Beck Hemp Mill near Pateley Bridge, issue day tickets.

The useful Northern *Angler's Handbook* covers details of all fishable waters and is on sale at bookshops and Yorkshire Dales National Park Information Centres.

Northumbrian Water
Northumbria House, Regent Centre, Gosforth, Newcastle NE3 3PX Tel: (01912) 843151 *River areas: Tyne, Aln, Coquet, Wansbeck.*

North-West Water plc,
Rivers Division, PO Box 12, New Town House, Buttermarket Street, Warrington WA1 2QG Tel: (01925) 53999 *River areas: Ribble, Lune and Eden.*

Ripley Castle Estate
Fishing by season ticket only.

Blackburn Farm Trout
Fishery, Gayle nr Hawes. Tel: (01969) 667524 *Fly fishing only.*

Kilnsey Water Park
see Country parks p182.

Hawes Angling Association
Tel: (01969) 667362 *15 miles of river fishing on the Ure for trout and grayling.*

Yorkshire Water plc
Amenity and Recreation Officer, Rivers Division, 21 Park Square South, Leeds.
Tel: (0113) 2440191
River areas: Aire, Wharfe, Nidd, Ure, Swale.

Golf Courses

Allendale
Alston Moor
Appleby
Barnard Castle
Bedale
Catterick
Clitheroe
Harrogate
Keighley
Knaresborough
Masham
Richmond
Sedbergh
Settle
Skipton
Whalley

White Hills Golf Driving Range
Stirton-with-Thorlby, Skipton
Tel: (01756) 793325

Horse Riding and Pony Trekking

Caton School of Equitation
Quernmore Road, Caton Lancaster
Tel: (01524) 770694

Fitton & Son
Bank Newton, Gargrave

Kilnsey Trekking Centre
Grassington
Tel: (01756) 752861

Sinderhope Pony Trekking Centre
Broadgate, Sinderhope, Allenheads, Northumbria NE47 9SH

West Park
Lunedale, Middleton-in-Teesdale, Co Durham

Long Distance Footpaths and Walks

The Calderdale Way
A walk following the approximate bounds of the Calder Valley watershed, linking public rights-of-way and permissive paths. Can be completed in five easy stages. 50 miles total length.

Coast to Coast Walk
From St Bees Head in Cumbria to Ravenscar on the Yorkshire Coast, crosses the Pennine way at Keld in upper Swaledale.

The Dales Way
A pleasant valley and fell walk of several days duration, starts at Ilkley in Wharfedale and finishes at Windermere.

The Ebor Way
Links the Dales Way and the Cleveland Way; passes through the historic city of York.

The Pennine Way
This route starts at Edale in Derbyshire and finishes at Kirk Yetholm in Scotland, passing through the area described in this book.

The Ribble Way
Follows the course of the Ribble, from the source to its estuary.

Market Days

Appleby - Saturday (cattle: Monday, Friday)
Barnard Castle - Wed.
Clitheroe - Tuesday, Saturday (cattle: Monday, Tuesday, Friday).
Gisburn - (cattle: Tuesday, Thursday)
Hawes - Tuesday
Ingleton - Friday
Kirkby Lonsdale - Thur.
Kirkby Stephen - Mon.

Knaresborough
Wednesday (cattle: Thursday)
Leyburn - Friday
Masham– Wed, Saturday
Middleton-in-Teesdale Tuesday
Reeth– Friday
Richmond - Saturday
Ripon - Thursday
Sedbergh - Wednesday (cattle: Friday)
Settle - Thursday
Skipton - Monday, Wednesday, Friday

Museums

Beamish North of England Open-Air Museum
Stanley, Co Durham, off A693. Stanley to Chester-le-Street road.
Tel: (01207) 231811
A 200-acre open-air museum of northern life, where buildings from the region have been rebuilt and furnished as they once were, with a 1920s town street with shops, houses, pub etc; a north-ern colliery with mine and pit cottages; a work-ing farm and a NER station and reconstructed steam locomotives. Working electric trams. *Open: Easter to mid-Sept., daily 10am-6pm; mid-Sept. to Easter, daily (except Mon.) 10am-5pm. Last admission always 4pm.*

Bedale Hall Museum
Bedale, DL8 1AA
Tel: (01677) 23131
Georgian ballroom with fine Italian plaster ceiling and rare scarfe jointed pine floor. Museum displays local art and crafts, trades-men's tools, clocks, coins, weights and many other interesting objects. 17th-century hall.
Open: May to Sept., 10am-4pm or by appointment.

Black Sheep Brewery plc.
Masham, North Yorks. HG4 4EN
Tel: (01756) 689227
Visitor Centre, brewery tours. *Open daily.*

Bowes Museum
Barnard Castle, ½ mile from town centre on Whorlton road. Collection of national importance housed in a French-style château. It includes paintings by El Greco and Goya and extensive collections of furniture, pottery, porcelain and tapestries. Administered by Durham County Council. *Open: every day, May to Sept.,10am-5.30pm; Oct., March and April 10am-5pm; Nov. to Feb., 10am-4pm: Sun., summer 2-5pm, winter 2-4pm. Closed one week Christmas and 1 January. Charge for admission.*

Brontë Parsonage and Museum
Haworth, Keighley. Many original manuscripts and personal memorabilia of the Brontë family.
Open: April to Sept., 11am-5.30pm; Oct. to March 11am-4.30pm; Closed 24, 25, 26 Dec. and for 3 weeks in Feb.

Brontë Weaving Shed
Townend Mill, Haworth, Keighley, West Yorkshire BD22 8EP
Tel: (01535) 646217
Edinburgh Woollen Mill collections combined with an exhibition in the form of a tribute to Timmy Feather, the last of Yorkshire's handloom weavers. Fully operating water wheel. *Open: Monday to Friday 10am-5.30pm. Saturday 10am-6pm. Sunday 11am-5pm.*

Clitheroe Castle Museum
Castle Hill, Clitheroe,
Lancs. Tel: (01200) 24635
or 25111
Small museum devoted
to life in the 19th
century. Museum
contains an important
collection of
carboniferous fossils and
a selection of items of
local significance.
*Open: Easter to October,
daily 2-4.30pm and Bank
Holidays 11am-4.30pm.*

Craven Museum
Town Hall, High Street,
Skipton.
Tel: (01756) 794079
Collection illustrating
history and archaeology
of Craven. *Open: April to
Sept., Monday, Wed.,
Thur. and Fri. 11am-5pm,
Sat. 10am-12noon and
1-5pm, Sunday 2-5pm;
Oct. to March, Mon.,
Wed., Thur. and
Fri. 2-5pm, Sat. 10am-
12noon & 1.30-4.40pm.
Closed Sundays and
Tuesdays.*

Dales Countryside Museum
Station Yard, Hawes.
Tel: (01969) 667450
Exhibition of life on
Dales' farm based on the
Marie Hartley and Joan
Ingilby collection.
Located in the goods
shed of the old railway
station. *Open: Easter or
1 April to September,
Monday to Saturday
11am-1pm and 2-5pm,
Sunday 2-5 pm; Oct.,
Tues., Sat. and Sun. only.*

Earby Museum of Mines
School Lane, Earby, on
A56, 6 miles south-west
of Skipton. A large col-
lection of Yorkshire Dales
lead mining equipment.
*Open: Thursday evenings
6-9pm and Sunday after-
noons 2-6pm.*

Georgian Theatre Royal and Theatre Museum
Victoria Road, Richmond.
General enquiries:
Tel: (01748) 823710
Box Office:
Tel: (01748) 823021
A unique fully
operational Georgian
theatre and adjacent
museum which links
modern productions
with 'the good old days'
through hand bills and
costumes, etc.
*Open: May to Sept.,
weekdays 2.30-5pm,
Saturday and Bank
Holiday Monday
10.30am-1.30pm.*

Green Howards Regimental Museum
Trinity Church Square,
Richmond.
Tel: (01748) 822133
Memorabilia of this
famous Yorkshire
regiment since its
formation in 1688. *Open:
April to Oct., weekday
9.30am-4.30pm, Sunday
2-4.30pm; Nov. and
March, Mon. to Sat.
10am-4.30pm; Feb.
Monday to Friday 10am-
4.30pm. Closed all Dec.
and Jan.*

Harrogate Art Gallery
Victoria Avenue,
Harrogate.
Tel: (01423) 503340
Permanent collection of
many fine oil and water
colour paintings,
including some by Turner
and Constable.

Ilkley Art Gallery and Museum
Ilkley, in centre of town.
Tel: (01943) 600066
Museum on the site of
Roman fort, and many
artefacts from this are
on display. *Open: daily
10am-6pm. Closed
Monday (except Bank
Holiday Mondays).*

Isurium
Boroughbridge off A1.
(Dere Street) 7 miles
south-east of Ripon.
Roman fort with several
preserved tesselated
pavements.
Small museum on site.

Killhope Wheel Lead Mining Centre
2½ miles west of
Cowshill on A689 in
Upper Weardale.
A restored lead crushing
mill, with a 34ft-high
waterwheel. The area's
best preserved lead
mining site. Exhibition
about lead mining and
life of the miner.
*Open: April, May, June
and Sept., daily (except
Mondays) 10.30am-5pm;
July and August, daily;
October weekends and
Wed.; Nov. to end of
March by appointment
for parties.*

Low Mill Museum
Bainbridge.
tel: (01969) 650416
Collection of local
artefacts.
*Open: Wed. and Bank
Holidays, 2-5pm. By
appointment only.*

Museum of Badges and Battledress
The Green, Crakehall,
nr Bedale, N. Yorks.
Private collection of
badges and uniforms
from 1900 to present day.
*Open: Easter to Sept.;
Tuesday to Friday 11am-
5pm; Saturday and
Sunday 1pm-5pm.*

Museum of North Craven Life
Victoria Street, Settle
Display of man in the
countryside around Settle
since prehistoric times.
Also temporary
exhibitions, guide cards,
demonstrations and
lectures.
*Open: May to June,
Saturday, Sunday 2-5pm;*
*July to September, daily
(except Monday) 2-5pm;
Oct. to April, Sat. 2-5pm.*

Museum of Steam
Caravan site off the
A682, 2 miles south of
Gisburn. Small collection
of steam driven vehicles,
including showman's
engines, all steamed
during the summer.
*Open: at all reasonable
times. Free admission.
Access for coaches.*

Nenthead Mines and Museum
A689, 5 miles south-east
of Alston. Reconstructed
mining area and
processing plant. Trails,
interpretive plaques.

Nentsberry Mining and Farming Museum
Open-air collection of
mining equipment, farm
implements. Narrow
gauge mine railway, play
area, picnic site.

Nidderdale Museum
Old Council Offices,
Pateley Bridge,
Nidderdale.
Tel: (01423) 711225
Recently enlarged with
several shop displays,
Victorian living room
and solicitor's office.
*Open: all year, every
Sun.; Easter to October,
weekends 2-5pm;
Whitsun to Oct., daily.*

Old Court House
Adjacent to
Knaresborough Castle
14th-century building
with a reconstructed
court room scene of 1602
including figures dressed
in period costume.
Tel: (01423) 503340

Old Court House Museum
Castle Yard,
Knaresborough.
Tel: (01423) 503340
Museum of local history
with original Tudor court.
*Open: 1 April to 30 Sept.;
Oct. to March, Sunday
only, 1.30-4.30pm.*

Richmondshire Museum
Ryders Wynd, Richmond
Tel: (01748) 825611
Museum of bygone
Richmond's county
before its amalgamation
with Yorkshire. Includes
the veterinary surgery
from the BBC production
of All Creatures Great
and Small, a story which
is set in the nearby dales.

Ripon Prison and Police Museum
St Marygate, Ripon.
Tel: (01765) 690799
Former Victorian prison
adapted to illustrate
crime and punishment
and law and order over
recent centuries.
*Open: Easter to Oct.;
weekdays (except
July/Aug.) 1-5pm; week-
days in July, Aug. and
Bank Holidays, 11am-
5pm, Sundays 1-5pm.*

Swaledale Folk Museum
Reeth Green, Reeth,
Swaledale.
Tel: (01748) 884373
(evenings only)
A museum of
agricultural life and
mining in bygone days
of this area.
*Open: Easter to Sept.,
daily 10.30am-6pm.*

Upper Wharfedale Museum
The Square, Grassington.
Tel: (01756) 752800
Displays of Dales' farm-
ing and industry of the
past; also included are
veterinary equipment
and a mineral collection.
*Open: April to Oct.,
daily 2-4.30pm.*

Wakeman's House Museum
Market Square, Ripon.
One-time home of the
wakeman, a medieval
guardian of the town.
The custom of blowing
the wakeman's curfew
horn is still maintained.
House is also an informa-
tion centre.
*Open: summer months
only and daylight hours.*

White Wells
Ilkley Moor.
Display of natural history
and geology. Accessible
only on foot.
*Open: summer, Saturday,
Sunday and Bank
Holiday Monday 2-6pm,
or by prior arrangement.*

Yorkshire Carriage Museum
Aysgarth Falls
Tel: (01969) 663399
Wensleydale, north of the
A684. One of the most
comprehensive collections
of horse drawn vehicles
used by the country
squire and his estate.

Museum of Yorkshire Poor Law
Ripon Workhouse,
Allhallowsgate, Ripon.
Tel: (01765) 690799
14 cells where tramps
were locked up at night.
Workyard and Hard
Times Gallery.
*Opening times as Prison
and Police Museum.*

Nature Reserves

Gouthwaite Reservoir Nature Reserve
Nidderdale, 4 miles
north-west of Pateley
Bridge. Bird sanctuary
not freely accessible to
general public, but many
birds can be seen from
the roads and trackways
surrounding the reservoir.

Grass Wood Nature Reserve
Wharfedale, 1½ mile
north-west of Grassington.
Ash woodland on
limestone. Owned and
maintained by the
Yorkshire Wildlife Trust
Ltd. Parties by
arrangement only.

Upper Teesdale National Nature Reserve
A botanically unique
area of 8,600 acres. The
area around Cauldron
Snout is accessible to the
general public and a
nature trail on
Widdybank Fell allows
visitors to see some of
the rare plants flowering
in their season.
Field studies are based at
Moor House.

Nature Trails

Aysgarth Falls Nature Trail
¼ mile east of Aysgarth,
(GR010887).
Nature trail starts from
National Park Centre and
follows wooded river
bank above a series of
attractive waterfalls.

Clapdale Wood
(Reginald Farrer Trust)
½ mile north of
Clapham.
Trail is in memory of
Reginald Farrer (1880-
1920), authority and
collector of Alpine
plants. Himalayan shrubs
and trees are featured in
the trail.

Gibson's Cave Nature Trail
Bowlees, Upper
Teesdale. Access from
B6277, 3 miles north-
west of Middleton-in-
Teesdale.
Nature trail starts from
Bowlees. Visitor Centre
car park and picnic area.
Interesting short walk
through wooded valley.

Ingleton's Waterfalls Walk
Follows a series of
natural waterfalls on the
River Greta.

Janet's Foss Woods
1 mile east of Malham
village, (SD912634).
Trail laid out with
explanatory plaques in
woodland below Janet's
Foss Waterfall.

Salthill Quarry Geological Trail
Near Clitheroe, Lancs.
Abandoned limestone
quarry with unique fossil
evidence. Nature
conservancy booklet
available.

Sedbergh Town Trail
Short interpretive walk
around Sedbergh.

Sedgwick Geological Trail
Lower Garsdale.
Short (1½ hour approx)
trail laid out on Longstone
Common, crosses Dent
Fault where the complex
folds of Lake District rocks
meet the horizontally
bedded Carboniferous
limestone and Yoredale
shales of the Pennine
Dales.
Trail in memory of Adam
Sedgwick (1785-1873)
father of modern geology.

Spring Wood Nature Trail
Whalley, near Clitheroe,
(SD741361). Mixed
woodland. Picnic site.

The Strid and Bolton Abbey Woods
Wharfedale, approached
from B6160, (SE077553).
Several trails of varying
length start and finish at
the Cavendish Pavilion.
Refreshments.

Valley Walks
Ilkley, Wharfedale.
Short waymarked routes
from ½ mile to 3½ miles.

Wheelhead Syke Nature Trail

Cow Green, off B6277 Upper Teesdale. Trail starts from scenic car park above Cow Green Reservoir. Open moorland, semi-alpine and tundra plants.

Organised Holidays and Courses

Birdguide
Ashville,
Rose Bank,
Burley in Wharfedale,
West Yorkshire LS29 7PQ

The Dales Centre
Grassington.
Tel: (01756) 752774

Malham Tarn Field Centre
Settle,
N. Yorks. BD24 9PU
Tel: (01729) 830331

HF Holidays Ltd
142 Great North Way,
London NW1 1EG
Tel: (0181203) 3381

Freetime Activities
Summer Lea, Joss Lane,
Sedbergh,
Cumbria LA10 5AS
Tel: (015396) 20828
Introduction to caving,
abseiling etc.

Swaledale Walking Guides Association
Tel: (01748) 825041

YHA
see Accommodation
p181.

Yorkshire Dales Adventure Centre Trust Ltd
Gildersleets, Giggleswick,
Settle.
Tel: (01729) 925359

Yorkshire Dales Guides
2 Moughton Villas,
Horton-in-Ribblesdale,
Settle,
N. Yorks. BD24 0HT
Tel: (01729) 860357

Other Places of Interest

Alston Market Cross
Alston, A686, 19 miles north-east of Penrith Covered market stand in main street. Highest market town in England.

Aysgarth Falls
$^1/_4$ mile east of Aysgarth. A series of stepped falls for 1 mile on either side of the Aysgarth to Carperby road.

Brimham Rocks
(National Trust) Near Pateley Bridge, access from B6265 or B6165. Moorland area dotted with natural sculptures made from weather-worn gritstone. Car park on perimeter. Trails indicated on information boards lead past most of the formations. Information centre and refreshments at Brimham House.

Buttertubs
On Thwaite to Hawes road, $2^1/_2$ miles south of Thwaite. Shallow pot-holes easily accessible from roadside. Car park and information panels.

Cauldron Snout Waterfall
Upper Teesdale, below Cow Green Reservoir. Access from Cow Green car park.

Dropping Well
Knaresborough
Tel: (01423) 862352
Petrifying well adjacent to Mother Shipton's Cave. Objects placed in the well are coated with stone over a period of several months.

Ebbing and Flowing Well
Buckhaw Brow, on A65. 1 mile north-west of Settle. (SD803654)

The Fall's Walk
Ingleton.Delightful wooded ravines and waterfalls. Footpath, steeply stepped in places makes an interesting 4 $^1/_2$ miles long circular walk. Small admission charge.

Fort Montague/House in the Rock
Knaresborough. 18th-century house carved from solid rock overlooking the River Nidd.
Open to the public during the summer months.

God's Bridge
2 miles west of Bowes on A77. Approach $^1/_4$ mile south of Pasture End Farm, (NY957127). Natural limestone bridge spanning River Greta.

Gordale Scar
$1^1/_2$ mile east of Malham village, SD915642. A deep limestone gorge formed by a collapsed cave system. Popular rock climbing area.

Hardraw Force
Access behind Green Dragon Inn, Hardraw, 1 mile north of Hawes, (SD868914). Highest above ground waterfall in England. Band concerts in summer. Small entry fee.

Hawes Ropeworks
Near to Station Yard, Hawes. A working ropeworks specialising in animal halters, church bell ropes, bannister and barrier ropes. Shop etc *Open: Monday to Friday 9am-5.30pm (closed $^1/_2$ hour lunch), Saturday in most school holidays, 10am-4pm (summer), closed Sunday.*

High Corn Mill
Mill Bridge, Skipton
Tel: (01756) 2883
Corn mill still using the power of two water-wheels. *Open: Wed., Sat. and Sunday 2-6pm.*

High Force
Upper Teesdale. Access from B6277 High Force Hotel, (NY881284) Small Fee.

Janet's Foss
1 mile east of Malham village, (SD912634). Cascade over a moss covered rock at the bottom of a wooded dell.

Kilnsey Crag
Wharfedale, $4^1/_2$ miles north-west of Grassington on B6160, (SD975679). Impressive overhanging limestone crag dominating the landscape.

Low Force
Upper Teesdale, on the B6277 1 mile N-west of Newbiggin. (NZ904279)

Malham Cove
$^1/_2$ mile north of Malham village, (SD896641). Natural limestone amphitheatre with water-worn pavement on high level. Remains of ancient field system below. Explanatory notices nearby.

Malham Tarn
2 miles north of village. A unique moorland lake and bird/nature sanctuary. Residential courses in all aspects of natural history run by the Field Studies Council at Malham Tarn Field Centre.

Norber Boulders
1 mile north-east of Clapham via A65. Silurian slate boulders left on white limestone

pedestals, by the retreating Ice Age glacier.

Ponden Mill
Colne Road,
Stanbury, Haworth,
West Yorkshire.
Tel: (01535) 643500
Unique retail complex in old woollen mill.

Ribblehead Viaduct
6 miles north-east of Ingleton near the B6255, (SD760795). Carries the Settle to Carlisle railway over some of the wildest upland country in England.

Shambles
Settle. Interesting group of old houses and shops on the east side of the market square. Naked Man Café on opposite side of street.

Stainforth Bridge and Force
(National Trust)
Below Stainforth on B6479, (SD817672). Elegantly arched packhorse bridge and attractive waterfall nearby.

The Strid
Wharfedale, 2 miles north-west of Bolton Abbey. (SE063565) Dramatic narrow cleft through which flows the River Wharfe. Many interesting water-worn rocks. Warning: Do not attempt to jump across The Strid, the river is very deep and fast.

Show Caves

Opening times can vary and often depend on the weather or the number of visitors. Check locally for up-to-date information.

Gaping Gill
3 miles north-east of Clapham. (SD751727) Local caving clubs organise winch descents,

Spring and August Bank Holidays.

Ingleborough Cave
1½ miles north of Clapham, approached by footpath through Clapdale Wood
Tel: (01524) 251242
Open: all year 10am-5pm; weekends only except bookings from Nov. to late February.

Mother Shipton's Cave
Knaresborough, on south bank of river, approached from B6163.
Tel: (01423) 862352
Reputed home of the 15th-century witch who prophesied many modern inventions.
Open most of the year.

Stump Cross Caverns
On B6265, Pateley Bridge to Grassington road, 5 miles west of Pateley Bridge. Easy access from road. Tel: (01756) 752780 Fine stalactite and stalagmite formations.
Visitor centre, café and gift shop.

White Scar Cave
1 mile north-east of Ingleton on B6255, access from road
Tel: (01524) 241244
Ample car parking.
Open: Feb. to Nov., daily, weather permitting.

Show Sports and Events

The exact dates vary each year and details should be checked with information centres. A weekly listing of activities taking place in Craven and around the Dales is published in the Craven News every Thursday under the heading 'Diary Dates'. Autumn shows take place at Wolsingham, Egglestone and Stanhope.

Allendale New Year's Eve Fire Ceremony, New Year's Eve.
Heptonstall Easter Pace Egg Play, Easter.
Three Peaks Race, April.
Gaping Gill Winch Descents, Bank Holidays.
Hardraw Band Contest, September.
Farm Open Days (check with National Park leaflet).
Arkengarthdale Sports and Sheep Show, May.
Street Market, Austwick, May.
Swaledale Festival, May.
Wensleydale Horse Show, May.
Tan Hill Sheep Show, May.
Pen-y-ghent Race and Gala, Horton-in-Ribblesdale, June.
Grassington Festival, June.
Appleby Horse Fair, June.
Hawes Sports (horses and sulkies), June.
Bainbridge Sports (motor-bikes), June.
Hawes Gala, June.
Masham, Great Traction Engine Rally and Steam Fair, mid-July.
Hebden Sports, August Bank Holiday Monday.
Malham Show, August.
Reeth Show, August.
Burnsall Sports, third Saturday August.
Grassington Exhibition, August.
Kilnsey Show, Tuesday after Bank Holiday Monday, August.
Leyburn Show, August Bank Holiday Saturday.
West Witton Feast and Burning of Bartle (St Bartholomew) Saturday nearest 24 Aug.
Upper Wharfedale Agricultural Show, August.
Wensleydale Agricultural Show, August.
Swaledale Agricultural Show, Muker, Sept.
Horton Show, September.

Morcock Show, Lunds, September.
Redmire Feast, September.
Nidderdale Agricultural Show, Pateley Bridge, September.
Three Peaks Cyclo-Cross, September.

Skiing

Cross Country
From Dufton Youth Hostel
Indoor Ski Slope
Catterick
Winter Ski Slopes
Allendale
Allenheads
Cross Fell
Upper Teesdale
Weardale
Westgate

Sport Centres

Coulthurst Craven Sports Centre
Sandylands,
Carleton New Road,
Skipton BD23 2AZ

Long Ashes Leisure Centre
Treshfield, nr Skipton,
N. Yorks BD23 5PW
Tel: (01756) 752780

Steam Railways

Keighley and Worth Valley Railway
Haworth Station,
Haworth, Keighley,
West Yorkshire.
Tel: (01535) 43629
(talking timetable)
Steam line operated by preservation society between Keighley British Rail Station and Oxenhope near Haworth.
Steam trains run every weekend, March to Oct., Bank Holidays and daily July and August.

South Tynedale Railway Preservation Society
Alston, on A686.
Narrow gauge railway along part of the old

branch line towards
Haltwhistle. Trains at
weekends Easter to
Sept.; daily during
summer. Shop, café,
tourist information,
parking at Alston
Station.

**Embsay and Bolton
Abbey Steam Railway**
Embsay, 1½ miles N.E of
Skipton, access from A59
Information and time
table: (01756) 710555
General enquiries:
(01756) 794727
Talking time table:
(01756) 795189
Short length of track and
good collection of steam
locomotives.
*Steam trains run on
Sundays and Bank
Holidays. Easter to Sept.,
plus Tuesday in July and
August. Also a number
of special events.*

Swimming Pools

Grassington
Upper Wharfedale
School
Ingleton
Heated open-air,
summer season.
Settle
Next to Settle middle
School
Skipton
Aireville Park

Tourist Information Centres

Information is also
available from the
Yorkshire and
Humberside Tourist
Board, Northumbrian
Tourist Board and North-
West Tourist Boards (see
under Accommodation
for addresses and
telephone numbers).

Barnard Castle
43 Galgate,
Tel: (01833) 690909

Bentham
Station Road,
Tel: (01524) 262549

Harrogate
Royal Baths Assembly
Rooms, Crescent Road,
Tel: (01423) 537300

Horton-in-Ribblesdale
Tel: (01729) 860333
Ingleton
Community Centre Car
Park,
Tel: (01524) 241049
Internet address:
www.yorkshirenet.co.uk/
ydales/ingleton

Ilkley
Tel: (01943) 602319

Kirkby Lonsdale
Tel: (015242) 71437

Leyburn
Thornborough Hall,
Tel: (01969) 623069

Pateley Bridge
Tel: (01423) 711147

Richmond
Friary Gardens,
Queens Road.
Tel: (01748) 850252

Settle
Town Hall
Tel; (01729) 825192

Skipton
9 Sheep St.
Tel: (01756) 792809

Useful Addresses

**British Mountaineering
Council**
Crawford House, Precinct
Centre, Booth Street East,
Manchester M13 9RZ
Tel: (0161273) 5835

**British Tourist Authority
Information Centre**
Lower Regent Street,
London W1

**Camping and
Caravanning Club**
11 Lower Grosvenor,
Place,
London SW1W 0EY
Tel: (0171828) 1012

Caravan Club
East Grinstead House,
East Grinstead,
Sussex RH19 1UA

Cyclists Touring Club
59 Meadrow,
Godalming,
Surrey GU7 3HS

English Heritage
PO Box 1BB
London W1A 1BB
Tel: (0171973) 3000

English Heritage
North Office,
Arnhem Block,
Carlisle Centre,
Carlisle CA3 8UR
Tel: (01228) 31777

National Trust
36 Queen Anne's Gate,
London, SW1 1HS
Tel: (0171222) 9251

Outward Bound Trust
Chestnut Field,
Regent Place,
Rugby CV21 2TJ
Tel: (01788) 60423/4/5

Ramblers Association
1-5 Wandsworth Road,
London SW8 2XX
Tel: (0171582) 6878

Yorkshire Wildlife Trust
20 Castlegate,
York YO1 1RP
Tel: (01904) 59570

Yorkshire Dales National Park Information Centres

Aysgarth Falls
Tel: (01969) 663424

Clapham
Tel: (01524) 251419

Colvend
Hebden Road,
Grassington, Skipton,

North Yorks. B23 5LB
Tel: (01756) 752748

Hawes
Upper Dales Folk
Museum,
Tel: (01969) 667450

Malham
Tel: (01729) 830363

Reeth
Tel: (01748) 884059

Sedbergh
Main Street,
Tel: (015396) 20125